STUDY GUIDE

FIFTH EDITION

INTRODUCTION TO

COMPUTERS &
INFORMATION SYSTEMS

THE INTERNET
EDITION

FIFTH EDITION

INTRODUCTION TO

COMPUTERS & INFORMATION SYSTEMS

Larry Long ■ Nancy Long

Prentice Hall, Upper Saddle River, New Jersey 07458

Acquisitions Editor: *Jo-Ann DeLuca*
Assistant Editor: *Audrey Regan*
Project Editor: *Genna Stefanelli*
Manufacturing Buyer: *Paul Smolenski*

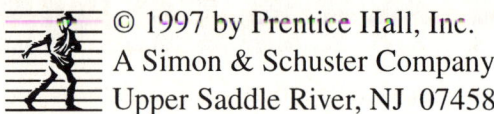 © 1997 by Prentice Hall, Inc.
A Simon & Schuster Company
Upper Saddle River, NJ 07458

Printed in the United States of America

10 9 8 7 6 5 4 3 2 1

ISBN 0-13-273228-9

Prentice-Hall International (UK) Limited, *London*
Prentice-Hall of Australia Pty. Limited, *Sydney*
Prentice-Hall Canada Inc., *Toronto*
Prentice-Hall Hispanoamericana, S.A., *Mexico*
Prentice-Hall of India Private Limited, *New Delhi*
Prentice-Hall of Japan, Inc., *Tokyo*
Simon & Schuster Asia Pte. Ltd., *Singapore*
Editora Prentice-Hall do Brasil, Ltda., *Rio de Janiero*

Contents

How to Use this Study Guide

The proliferation of computers in the business world has made an understanding of computers and computer applications an important consideration for any career-oriented person. This *Study Guide* is intended to complement *Introduction to Computers and Information Systems: Internet Edition*, by Larry Long and Nancy Long (Prentice Hall, 1997). It complements the text in a manner that will help make your learning about computers a more meaningful and rewarding experience. The *Study Guide* is written with these objectives in mind:

- To support and reinforce the material presented in *Introduction to Computers and Information Systems: Internet Edition*.
- To provide a means of evaluating how well you understand the concepts presented in the text.

The *Study Guide* contains the following for each chapter/appendix.

- *Student Learning Objectives* These objectives provide insight into what you should expect to learn.
- *Vocabulary Study* The vocabulary study summarizes the key terms in the chapter.
- *Interactive Review* The interactive review is a fill-in-the-blank review of the text material that tests your grasp of key terms and concepts in the chapter. The terms are presented within the context of a chapter summary. All terms are in the Vocabulary Study and appear in the text as **bold** face terms. Note that the number of words and letters contained in each term is depicted by the appropriate number of underscores in the Interactive Review.
- *Practice Test* This section offers you an opportunity to test your knowledge of the material and to familiarize yourself with the types of multiple-choice, true/false, and matching questions you might expect on a test. Answers to the Practice Test follow the matching questions.
- *Chapter Checkup* Use the space provided to respond to a variety of question types that may call for synthesis of chapter concepts, personal opinion, recall, association, generation of test questions, and so on. Many questions on chapter concepts refer you to the page(s) in the main text that contains the answer or related information. The last few questions in this section refer to the special-interest sidebars in the chapter. You might be interested to know that the amount of information you retain after hearing and/or reading it is only a shadow of what you retain after writing the information down.
  The Chapter Checkup is designed such that your instructor has the flexibility to assign it as a hand-in exercise.
- *Graphical User Interface* The Graphical User Interface uses visual association to challenge your understanding of selected computer terms, components, or concepts discussed in the chapter.

We wish you good luck in your computer adventure,

Larry Long
Nancy Long
Henry Rowe

**Chapter 1
The World of Computers**

STUDENT LEARNING OBJECTIVES

- To grasp the scope of computer understanding needed by someone living in an information society.
- To describe the implications of computer networks on organizations and on society.
- To demonstrate awareness of the relative size, scope, uses, and variety of available computer systems.
- To describe the fundamental components and the operational capabilities of a computer system.
- To identify and describe uses of the computer.

VOCABULARY STUDY

backup
bulletin-board system (BBS)
CD-ROM
CD-ROM drive
chip
client computer
communications software
computer
computer competency
computer network
computer system
computer-aided design (CAD)
computer-based training (CBT)
computerese
configuration
cyberphobia
data
database software
desktop PC
desktop publishing software
disk
docking station
download
downtime
edutainment software
electronic mail (e-mail)
enterprise-wide system
floppy disk drive
floppy diskette
graphics software
hard copy
hard disk drive

hardware
host computer
information
information service
information society
information superhighway
information system
information technology (IT)
input
input/output (I/O)
input/output-bound
integrated circuit
keyboard
knowledge worker
laptop PC
local area network (LAN)
mainframe computer
master file
microcomputer (micro)
microsecond
millisecond
minicomputer (mini)
monitor
mouse
multimedia application
nanosecond
National Information
Infrastructure (NII)
notebook PC
offline
online
output

palmtop PC
pen-based PC
peripheral device
personal computer (PC)
personal computing
personal digital assistant (PDA)
picosecond
pocket PC
printer
process and device control
processor
processor-bound
program
random-access memory (RAM)
record
resolution
server computer
soft copy
software
spreadsheet software
supercomputer
terminal
the Internet (the Net)
tower PC
upload
uptime
user
video display terminal (VDT)
word processing software
workstation

INTERACTIVE REVIEW

Use the terms in the Vocabulary Study to fill in the following blanks. You will only use each term once. You may need to insert a plural form of a term or adjust its verb tense. Check your answers with the chapter material and the glossary in your textbook.

1-1

The computer revolution has spawned an _____ _____ filled with _____ _____ who focus their energies on providing a cornucopia of information services.

Millions of people can be "at work" wherever they are as long as they have their portable _____ _____ (PCs) at a client's office, in an airplane, or at home. The mobile worker's __ (personal computer) enables electronic links to a vast array of information and to clients and corporate colleagues. Even the way we communicate with each other has changed. _____ _____ and _____ _____ _____ (____) are just two of the tools we use for computer communications. In fact, we owe a lot of the improvement in our standard of living over the past twenty years to the computer, and the future promises to be even more exciting. The _____ _____ _____ (___) or _____ _____, as it is often refered to, is a futuristic network of high-speed data communication links, primarily fiber optic technology, that eventually will connect virtually every facet of our society. This technology involves the integration of this high-speed data communications network with computer and television technologies.

The first electronic computer emerged on the scene about 50 years ago. In the early days of commercial computers, a computer professional served as an intermediary between the user someone who uses a computer and the computer system. Today, at the corporate level, virtually every business has embraced _____ _____ (__) and are using IT to offer better services and gain a competitive advantage. To fully appreciate information and its relation to information technology, we must also examine its origin. _____ (the plural of datum) are the raw materials from which information is derived. _____ is data that have been collected and processed into a meaningful form. Traditionally, we have thought of data in terms of numbers (account balance) and letters (customer name), but recent advances in information technology have opened the door to data in other formats such as images and sounds. For example, dermatologists (physicians who specialize in skin disorders) use digital cameras to take close-up pictures of patients' skin disorders. Each patient's _____ (information about the patient) on the computer-based _____ _____ (all patient records) is then updated to include the digital image.

In less than a generation, _____ _____ has emerged in virtually every career from a nice-to-have skill to a job-critical skill. Anyone suffering from _____ will soon find it next to impossible to function effectively in modern society. To be computer competent, an individual must be comfortable with computers. A person needs to know how to use computers for problem solving and generate _____ to the computer and interpret _____ from it. One must understand the impact of computers on society, now and in the future. One must be able to intelligently purchase computer _____ and other computer-related products. One also needs a basic knowledge of various computer _____ products. Software is the term used to describe a computer _____ which are the instructions that enable a computer to function. One must also be conversant in _____ , the language of computers and information technology.

1-2

Survival in the new global economy depends on the rapid and free flow of information to and from all corners of the globe. The _ _ _ _ _ _ _ _ _ _ _ _ _ _ has been instrumental in this and has allowed people to work together with computers on a worldwide scale. A global network called _ _ _ _ _ _ _ _ _ _ _ connects more than 40,000 networks, millions of large multiuser computers, and tens of millions of users in more than 100 countries. One way to access _ _ _ _ _ _ (the Internet) is to subscribe to a commercial _ _ _ _ _ _ _ _ _ _ _ _ _ _ _ _ _ _ , such as America Online, CompuServe, or Prodigy. Users go _ _ - _ _ _ _ with information networks to obtain desired services and data. Processing and manipulation of data received from an on-line service can usually be done _ _ _ - _ _ _ _ or after the link is terminated. Surfers on the Internet desiring to read a story or listen to a song, _ _ _ _ _ _ _ _ the text or a digitized version of a song to their personal computer, then read it or play it through. Information is _ _ _ _ _ _ from a local computer to a remote computer.

1-3

The _ _ _ _ _ _ _ _ is an electronic device that can interpret and execute programmed commands for input, output, computation, and logic operations. The computeer or _ _ _ _ _ _ _ _ _ , is the "intelligence" of a _ _ _ _ _ _ _ _ _ _ _ _ _ . It performs all computation and logic operations. Output from a computer can take many forms. The output on a _ _ _ _ _ _ _ is temporary and is called _ _ _ _ _ _ _ _ . The use of a device such as a _ _ _ _ _ _ _ is required for _ _ _ _ _ _ _ _ output. Data can be entered to a computer system for processing (input) via a _ _ _ _ _ _ _ _ (one character at a time), a microphone (for voice and sound input), or a point-and-draw devices such as a _ _ _ _ _ _ . A computer uses _ _ _ _ _ _ - _ _ _ _ _ _ _ _ _ _ _ _ (_ _ _) for temporary storage of data and programs during processing within solid state _ . The term _ _ _ _ _ _ is used to refer to these integrated circuits which are small squares of silicone with thousands of electronic components etched into them. Permanently installed and interchangeable _ _ _ _ _ provide permanent storage for data and programs.

Computers can be found in a variety of shapes and sizes. _ _ _ _ _ _ _ _ _ _ _ _ _ _ _ _ _ _ have greater computing capacities than do personal computers, which are also called _ _ _ _ _ _ _ _ _ _ _ _ _ _ _ _ (or _ _ _ _ _ _ _). _ _ _ _ _ _ _ _ _ _ _ _ _ _ _ _ , the biggest of all, have greater computing capacities than do mainframe computers. Depending on its sophistication, a _ _ _ _ _ _ _ _ _ _ _ _ _ _ _ ' computing capacity falls somewhere between that of a micro and a midsized mainframe. All computers, no matter how small or large, have the same fundamental capabilities_input, processing, output, and storage. Micros, workstations, mainframes, and supercomputers are computer systems. Each offers many _ _ _ _ _ _ / _ _ _ _ _ _ _ or _ / _ alternatives -- ways to enter data to the system and to present information generated by the system.

1-4

Personal computers come in four different physical sizes: _ _ _ _ _ _ _ _ _ , _ _ _ _ _ _ _ _ _ _ , _ _ _ _ _ _ _ _ _ _ , and _ _ _ _ _ _ _ _ . The pocket PC, sometimes called a _ _ _ _ _ _ _ _ _ _ , literally can fit in a coat pocket or a handbag. Laptops, which weigh from four to eight pounds, are often called _ _ _ _ _ _ _ _ _ _ _ because they are about the size of a one-inch thick notebook. Desktop PCs and tower PCs are not designed for frequent movement and, therefore, are not considered portable. The power of a PC is not necessarily directly related to its size. A few laptop PCs can run circles around some desktop PCs. Some user conveniences, however, must be sacrificed to achieve portability. The 2-in-1 PC can be used as a notebook and can use a _ _ _ _ _ _ _ _ _ _ _ _ _ to function as a desktop PC. A computer system's _ _ _ _ _ _ _ _ _ _ _ _ _ describes its internal components (for example, size of RAM and special features) and its _ _ _ _ _ _ _ _ _ _ _ _ _ _ _ _ _ _ _ (printer, various disk storage devices, monitor, and so on). Mobile workers in increasing numbers are using portable _ _ _ - _ _ _ _ _ _ _ that use electronic pens instead of keyboards. The _ _ _ _ _ _ _ _

(_ _ _ _) are hand-held personal computers, like palmtop and pen-based computers, and are also often called personal communicators.

It is important that you know what makes up a microcomputer system and how it fits together. Nowadays, the typical off-the-shelf PC is configured to run _ that combine text, sound, graphics, motion video, and/or animation. The typical multimedia-configured micro includes a microcomputer, a keyboard for input, a point-and-draw device for input, a monitor for soft-copy (temporary) output, a printer for hard-copy (printed) output, a permanently installed high-capacity _ _ _ _ _ _ _ _ _ _ _ _ for permanent storage of data and programs, a low-capacity _ _ _ _ _ _ _ _ _ _ _ _ _ _ into which an interchangeable _ _ _ _ _ _ _ _ _ _ _ _ _ _ is inserted, a high-capacity _ _ - _ _ _ _ _ _ _ _ into which an interchangeable _ _ - _ _ _ , which looks like an audio CD, is inserted, a microphone (audio input), and a set of speakers (audio output).

The PC was fine for word processing, spreadsheets, and games, but real "power users," engineers doing _ _ _ _ _ _ _ _ _ - _ _ _ _ _ _ _ _ _ _ , or _ _ _ , scientists, and other "number crunchers" need the power and speed of a workstation. The workstation's input/output devices also set it apart from a PC. The quality of a monitor's output is a function of its _ _ _ _ _ _ _ _ _ _ _ , the clarity of the image on the monitor's display. A workstation can also use a variety of point-and-draw devices and add-on keypads. The capabilities of today's high-end PCs are very similar to those of low-end workstations.

Mainframe computers are usually associated with _ _ _ _ _ _ _ _ _ _ - _ _ _ _ _ _ _ _ _ _ that service entities throughout the company . Users communicate with a centralized mainframe, called a _ _ _ _ _ _ _ _ _ _ _ _ , through their _ _ _ _ _ _ _ _ _ _ _ _ _ _ _ _ _ _ _ (_ _ _), or simply _ _ _ _ _ _ _ _ . Depending on the size of the organization, a dozen people or 10,000 people can share system resources by interacting with their VDTs. In the late 1960s, computer vendors introduced smaller, _ _ _ _ _ _ _ _ _ _ _ _ _ _ _ or simply _ _ _ _ _ that were more affordable for smaller companies. Today the distinction between minis and mainframes is rather blurred and the term is seldom used. Smaller mainframes are called midsized computers. Mainframes are oriented to _ _ _ _ _ _ / _ _ _ _ _ _ _ - _ _ _ _ _ applications; that is, the amount of work that can be performed by the computer system is limited primarily by the speeds of the I/O and storage devices. Supercomputers are considered to be _ _ _ _ _ _ _ _ _ _ - _ _ _ _ _ because the amount of work that can be done by the computer system is limited primarily by the speed of the computer. Supercomputers are known as much for their applications as they are for their speed or computing capacity, which may be 10 times that of a large mainframe computer.
1-5

A _ _ _ _ _ _ _ _ _ _ _ _ _ _ _ _ _ _ _ (_ _ _) connects PCs in close proximity, such as in a suite of offices or a building. In most LANs, a _ _ _ _ _ _ _ _ _ _ _ _ _ performs a variety of functions for the other PCs on the LAN called _ _ _ _ _ _ _ _ _ _ _ _ _ _ _ . One of the functions of a server computer may include the storage of data and applications software. A source document is the original document from which data are entered by data entry personnel. In a typical payroll system, the data are stored on the server computer's personnel master file. Each employee has a _ _ _ _ _ _ _ on the master file that contains name, hours worked, year-to-date FICA contribution, and other pertinent personnel data. The master file and individual records can be used by a number of different programs to produce a variety of output.

The computer reads from input and storage devices. The computer writes to output and storage devices. Before data can be processed, they must be "read" from an input device or data storage device. The computer is totally objective. It can perform only computation and logic operations. Computation operations are addition (+), subtraction (-), multiplication (*), division (/), and exponentiation (^). Logic operations are comparisons between numbers and between words. Computers are fast, accurate, consistent, and reliable. Computers perform various activities by executing instructions. These operations are measured in _ _ _ _ _ _ _ _ _ _ _ _ ,

_ _ _ _ _ _ _ _ _ _ _ _ _ , _ _ _ _ _ _ _ _ _ _ _ _ , and _ _ _ _ _ _ _ _ _ _ _ (one thousandth, one millionth, one billionth, and one trillionth of a second, respectively. Computations by a computer are accurate within a penny, a micron, a picosecond, or whatever level of precision is required. Computers always do what they are programmed to do, nothing more, nothing less. Anything below 99.9% _ _ _ _ _ _ for a computer, the time when the computer system is in operation, is usually unacceptable. For some companies, any _ _ _ _ _ _ _ _ is unacceptable. These companies provide _ _ _ _ _ _ computers that take over automatically should the main computers fail. Computer systems have total and instant recall of data and an almost unlimited capacity to store these data.

1-6

The uses of computers are like the number of melodies available to a songwriter_limitless. If you can imagine it, there is a good chance that computers can help you do it. The bulk of existing computer power is dedicated to _ _ _ _ _ _ _ _ _ _ _ _ _ _ _ _ _ _ _ . This category includes all uses of computers that support the administrative aspects of an organization. We combine hardware, software, people, procedures, and data to create an information system. The growth of _ _ _ _ _ _ _ _ _ _ _ _ _ _ _ _ _ , an environment in which one person controls the PC, has surpassed even the most adventurous forecasts of a decade ago. Some companies actually have more personal computers than telephones. _ enables users to enter and edit text in documents in preparation for output. _ allows users to produce near-typeset-quality copy for newsletters, advertisements, and many other printing needs, all from the confines of a desktop. _ _ _ _ _ _ _ _ _ _ _ _ _ _ _ _ _ permits users to work with the rows and columns of a matrix (or spreadsheet) of data. _ _ _ _ _ _ _ _ _ _ _ _ _ _ _ _ permits users to create and maintain a database and to extract information from the database. _ _ _ _ _ _ _ _ _ _ _ _ _ _ _ _ facilitates the creation and management of computer-based images consisting of just about anything that can be drawn in the traditional manner. _ _ _ _ _ _ _ _ _ _ _ _ _ _ lets users send e-mail and faxes, tap the Internet, log on to an information service, or link their PC with a remote computer and computer networks. Engineers and scientists routinely use the computer as a tool in experimentation, design, and development.

Computers can interact with students to enhance the learning process. Computer-based education will not replace teachers, but educators agree that _ _ _ _ _ _ _ _ - _ _ _ _ _ _ _ _ _ _ _ _ _ (_ _ _) is having a profound impact on traditional modes of education. Computer-aided design (CAD) is using the computer in the design process. CAD systems enable the creation and manipulation of an on-screen graphic image. More applications are being created that tickle our fancy and entertain us. Software developers are going even further by developing _ _ _ _ _ _ _ _ _ _ _ _ _ _ _ _ that combines education aspects of a subject with entertainment activities.

In the years ahead, look for personal computing, workgroup computing, education, and artificial intelligence to become larger shares of a growing computer "pie." Your participation and most assuredly your success in the world to come will be directly related to your ability to interact effectively with information systems.

PRACTICE TEST

Multiple Choice *Circle the most appropriate answer.*

1. The term "intelligence of a computer system" refers to the
   a. computer's keyboard.
   b. computer system's magnetic disk.
   c. computer's processor.
   d. computer's internal VDT.

2. "When Pay > 250 then print report" is an example of which computer operation?
   a. logic
   b. output registers
   c. division
   d. computation

3. "Total + Commission = Pay" is an example of which computer operation?
   a. division
   b. output registers
   c. logic
   d. computation

4. The programs that cause the computer to perform desired functions are called
   a. specifications.
   b. software.
   c. data.
   d. hardware.

5. The presentation of the results of computer processing is referred to as
   a. a master file.
   b. output.
   c. an information network.
   d. edutainment.

6. Cyberphobia is the irrational fear of
   a. computers.
   b. robots.
   c. persons who wear digital wristwatches.
   d. the color cyan.

7. Using the computer in the industrial design process is referred to as
   a. EFT.
   b. CAP.
   c. CAM.
   d. CAD.

8. Which of the following is not an operational capability of a computer system?
   a. processing operations
   b. input operations
   c. register highlighting
   d. output operations

9. Mainframe computers are oriented to input/output-bound operations, which means
   a. the amount of work that can be done is limited by the peripheral devices.
   b. they can accommodate keyboard entry only.
   c. that the operator console must be very large.
   d. that the down time is greater than for microcomputers.

10. Data that you copy directly into your computer from another computer is said to be
   a. inloaded.   c. outloaded.
   b. downloaded.   d. uploaded.

11. Computer output produced by a printer is commonly called
    a.   a source document.
    b.   soft copy.
    c.   a master document.
    d.   hard copy.
12. A 2 in 1 PC can function as a desktop PC by inserting it into a
    a.   service station.
    b.   workstation.
    c.   docking station.
    d.   terminal station.

True - False *Circle T for true and F for false.*

13.   T F   A VDT is an input device for a personal computer.
14.   T F   Data are to a computer system as gas is to an automobile.
15.   T F   Computer input is information that is to be processed into meaningful data.
16.   T F   The computer can perform both logic and computation operations.
17.   T F   A nanosecond is one billionth of a second.
18.   T F   CAD is the most sophisticated implementation of a knowledge-based system.
19.   T F   We are in transition from an industrial society to an information society.
20.   T F   Personal computers are also called mainframe computers.
21.   T F   CBT allows for self-paced learning in educational computer applications.
22.   T F   Microcomputers are often called personnel computers, or PCs, because of their extensive use in the personnel placement industry.
23.   T F   The printer is not considered an input device to a computer system.
24.   T F   When discussing computers, the term downtime refers to the period of time when a processor bound computer system is processing data and will not accept input.
25.   T F   The acronym LAN stands for log-on area network.
26.   T F   RAM is a form of temporary data storage.
27.   T F   Minicomputers are functionally the same as personal computers.
28.   T F   Keyboards, printers, and monitors are also called peripheral devices.
29.   T F   The enterprise-wide information system is typically a company's secondary source of information.
30.   T F   Microcomputers are functionally the same as personal computers.

Matching *Match the following terms with the appropriate definition or characteristic by placing the letter of the matching definition or characteristic in the blank.*

31. _____ information system

32. _____ server computer

33. _____ picosecond

34. _____ personal computer

35. _____ hard copy

36. _____ word processing

37. _____ master file

38. _____ natural language software

39. _____ VDT

40. _____ uptime

41. _____ processor

42. _____ output

(a) Enables computer systems to accept, interpret, and execute instructions in the native language of the user

(b) A software productivity tool for text manipulation

(c) Performs a variety of functions for other computers on a LAN

(d) A label associated with the microcomputer because it was designed for use by one person at a time

(e) Data that have been processed into information

(f) Combining software, hardware, people, procedures and data

(g) A type of computer terminal

(h) Another word for computer

(i) One trillionth of a second

(j) A readable printed copy of computer output

(k) A permanent source of data for a computer application

(l) When the computer is operational

Answers to Practice Test **1** c, **2** a, **3** d, **4** b, **5** b, **6** a, **7** d, **8** c, **9** a, **10** b, **11** d, **12** c, **13** f, **14** t, **15** f, **16** t, **17** t, **18** f, **19** t, **20** f, **21** t, **22** f, **23** t, **24** f, **25** f, **26** t, **27** f, **28** t, **29** f, **30** t, **31** f, **32** c, **33** i, **34** d, **35** j, **36** b, **37** k, **38** a, **39** g, **40** l, **41** h, **42** e.

CHAPTER CHECKUP

NAME		DATE	CHAPTER 1
COURSE	SECTION	INSTRUCTOR	

1. The computer revolution is definitely upon us and affects both our private lives and our professional lives. Glance through the photos in Chapter 1 of the text, identify and describe three photos that show how computers are being used in either a person's private life or in a business environment. *Computers have permeated into all areas of our lives. Every aspect of the business world uses computers in some way and our personal lives interact with computers regularly, oftentimes, when we don't even realize it.*

-

-

-

2. Describe yourself in terms of your knowledge and use of computers. *You can include such terms as cyberphobic, end user, user, computer professional, hacker, computer illiterate, computer competent, and so on.*

3. Think of two situations where the timeliness of information is of paramount importance, and list them here. *For example: Hospital emergency information or stock market quotes.*

-

-

4. What type of information could be produced from the data entered by retail clerks at a grocery store? *Think of all the functions involved in operating a successful retail business. These range from the basics of keeping the shelves stocked and items correctly priced to maintaining a competent staff of employees and even security.*

5. Identify the four components of a computer system and give an example of each. *See Figure 1-4 in the text. The payroll system illustrated in Figure 1-7 shows how data are entered and how the four computer components interact to produce information.*

■

■

■

■

6. Enter the terms that identify each of the following time periods: one-billionth of a second, one-thousandth of a second, one-trillionth of a second, and one-millionth of a second. *Do you remember what all the terms are: millisecond-nanosecond-microsecond-picosecond? See section 1-5 of the text.*

■

■

■

■

7. How would you define an information system? *Don't confuse an information system with a computer system. See section 1-6 of the text.*

8. List five popular microcomputer productivity tools mentioned in the chapter and a function of each. *One helps you write letters and another helps you create images.*

■

■

■

■

■

9. What four fundamental components do all computer systems have in common? *Something goes in, then it is manipulated, saved, and presented for us to interpret.*

■

■

■

■

10. Summarize the author's main points concerning computer competency you should learn upon completing this course. *The author has listed seven points. See section 1-1 of the text.*

■

■

■

■

■

■

■

11. If you were to use an information network, what type of information service (for example, airline reservations, stock quotations, etc.) would be of greatest interest to you? *There are several examples described in the text and a lot more that space wouldn't permit. See section 1-2 of the text.*

12. List any electronic bulletin boards with which you are familiar or use. *See section 1-1 and section 1-2 of the text.*

13. Look around the room in which you are sitting and list as many items as you can that might have a microprocessor. If there are none, where would you go to find one and what item(s) did you find? *Don't forget the telephone or how about your watch?*

14. What advantages does a laptop PC have over a pocket PC? How about a desktop PC over a laptop PC? *See section 1-4 of the text.*

15. What hardware components would be included in a typical microcomputer configuration? *See section 1-4 of the text.*

16. List one application for supercomputers listed in the text and one of your own. *In Michael Crichton's book,* Jurassic Park, *scientists needed the power of three supercomputers to create the DNA structures they needed to clone dinosaurs.*

-

-

17. List three clues that distinguish a PC from a workstation. *See section 1-4 of the text.*

-

-

-

18. Explain the relationships between data, information, input, and output as these terms relate to computers and information systems. *Remember which is derived from the other, and which term can easily be synonomyous whith one another. See section 1-5 of the text.*

19. List the components found in a typical multimedia microcomputer system. *The textbook lists ten. See section 1-4 of the text.*

-
-
-
-
-

-
-
-
-
-

20. Compose a multiple-choice, a true/false, and an essay question that you think would be appropriate for a quiz on this chapter.
Hint: The Review Exercises and Self-Test at the end of the chapter offer many good examples of each type of question.

M/C:
(a)
(b)
(c)
(d)
T/F:
Essay:

GRAPHICAL USER INTERFACE

Name the computer hardware items pictured below.

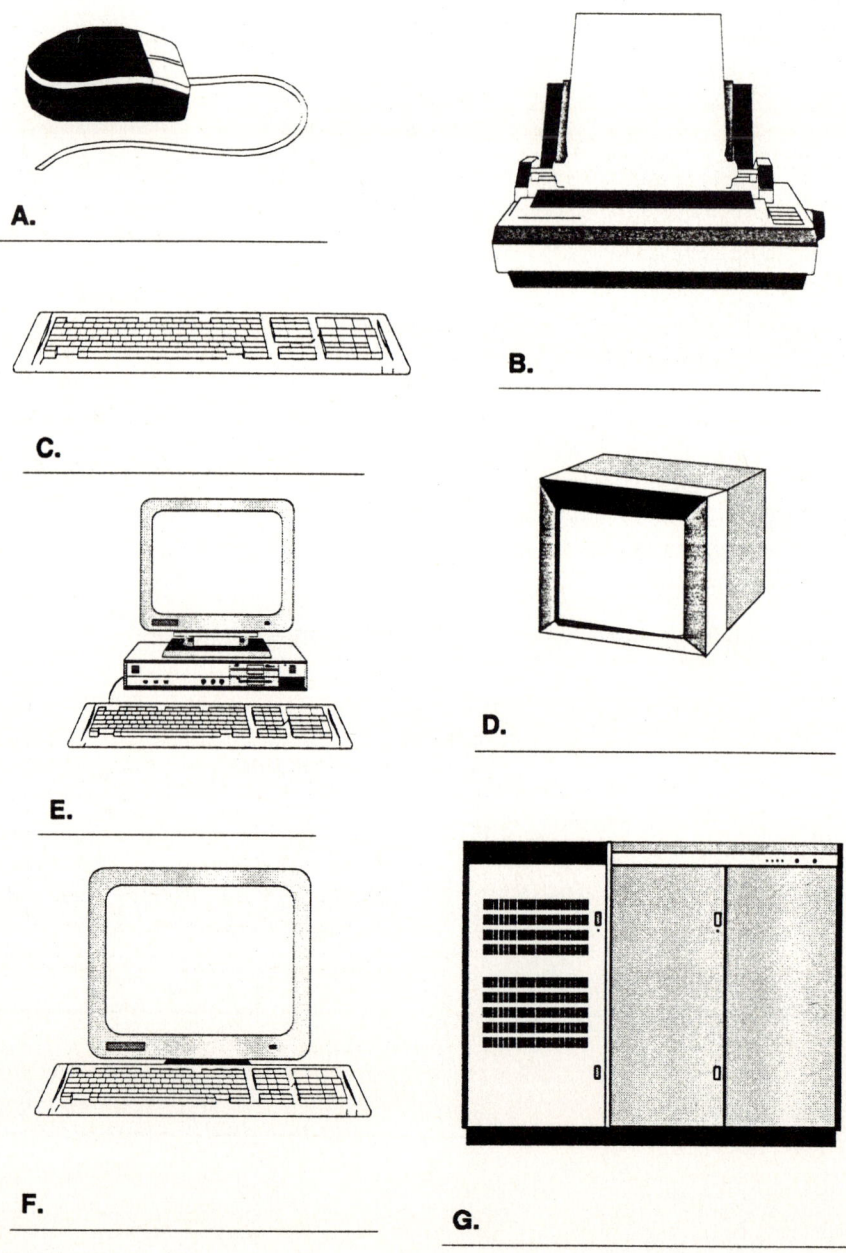

A. _____

B. _____

C. _____

D. _____

E. _____

F. _____

G. _____

GRAPHICAL USER INTERFACE

Identify each of the following personal computers and rank them 1 (smallest) through 4.

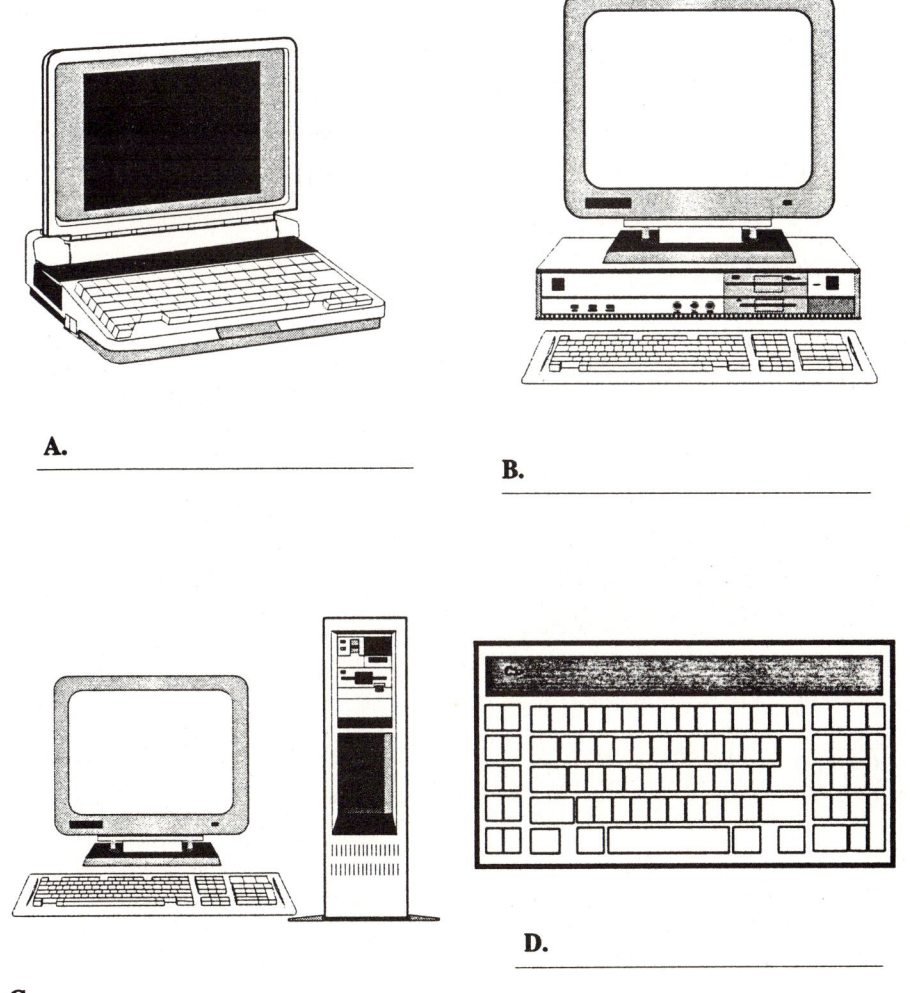

A. _____

B. _____

C. _____

D. _____

Chapter 2
Inside the Computer

STUDENT LEARNING OBJECTIVES

- To describe how data are stored in a computer system.
- To demonstrate the relationships between bits, bytes, characters, and encoding systems.
- To understand the translation of alphanumeric data into a format for internal computer representation.
- To explain and illustrate the principles of computer operations.
- To distinguish processors by their word size, speed, and memory capacity.
- To identify and describe the relationships between the internal components of a personal computer.

VOCABULARY STUDY

accumulator
address
address bus
alpha
alphanumeric
analog
ANSI
arithmetic and logic unit
ASCII
binary
bit
bubble memory
bus
byte
cache memory
carrier
central processing unit (CPU)
Centronics connector
CISC
control unit
data bus
decoder
device controller
digital
digitize
dynamic RAM (DRAM)
encoding system
execution time (E-time)
expansion board
expansion bus

expansion card
expansion slot
extended ASCII
facsimile (fax)
fax modem
flash memory
FLOPS
GFLOPS
gigabytes (GB)
instruction register
instruction time (I-time)
kilobits (Kb)
kilobytes (KB)
local bus
machine cycle
machine language
massively parallel processing
(MPP)
megabits (Mb)
megabytes (MB)
megahertz (MHz)
microprocessor
MIPS
modem
motherboard
multifunction expansion board
nondestructive read
nonvolatile memory
numeric
P6

parallel port
parallel processing
PCI local bus
PCMCIA card (PC card)
Pentium (microprocessor)
platform
port
PowerPC (microprocessor)
primary storage
program register
programmable read-only memory
(PROM)
register
RISC
RS-232C connector
SCSI bus
secondary storage
serial port
single in-line memory modules
(SIMMs)
static RAM (SRAM)
system board
terabytes (TB)
throughput
Unicode
VL-bus
volatile memory
word

INTERACTIVE REVIEW

Use the terms in the Vocabulary Study to fill in the following blanks. You will only use each term once. You may need to insert a plural form of a term or adjust its verb tense. Check your answers with the chapter material and the glossary in your textbook.

2-1

Electronically, _ _ _ _ _ _ signals are continuous wave forms that can be used to represent such things as sound, temperature, and velocity. In contrast, our audio compact disks (CDs) store and transmit music in _ _ _ _ _ _ _ format, that is, in strings of 1s and 0s. The music industry _ _ _ _ _ _ _ _ _ the natural analog signals that result from recording sessions, then stores the digital version on CDs. There are two basic electronic states, on and off. In computers, each of these states are represented by one of two _ _ _ _ , the on-bit and the off-bit (written as one and zero). Thus, the language of computers is written using the _ _ _ _ _ _ numbering system. Data are stored temporarily in _ _ _ _ _ _ _ _ _ _ _ _ _ _ and permanently in _ _ _ _ _ _ _ _ _ _ _ _ _ _ _ _ . Data stored in either of these must be in a form that the computer can understand.

2-2

An _ _ _ _ _ _ _ _ _ _ _ _ _ _ _ _ is used to translate the _ _ _ _ _ characters, _ _ _ _ _ _ _ characters, and special characters that people use to communicate computer instructions into binary form. Alpha and numeric characters are referred to collectively as _ _ _ _ _ _ _ _ _ _ _ _ _ characters. The seven-bit _ _ _ _ _ code can be used to represent 128 characters (a character in computer terminology is usually a _ _ _ _ _ .) _ _ _ _ _ _ _ _ _ _ _ _ _ , an 8-bit code, can be used to represent up to 256 separate characters. _ _ _ _ is an eight-bit code used by Microsoft Windows. Several computer hardware and software companies are sponsoring the development of the 16-bit _ _ _ _ _ _ _ that can represent up to 65,536 characters.

2-3

The _ , or _ _ _ for short, has only two fundamental sections, the control unit and the arithmetic and logic unit. Data are input to the CPU from RAM. RAM is all electronic and has no moving parts. Physically, memory chips are installed on _ _ _ _ _ _ _ _ -_ _ _ _ _ _ _ _ _ _ _ _ _ _ _ _ _ or _ _ _ _ _ . The most common RAM technologies are _ _ _ _ _ _ _ _ _ _ _ (_ _ _ _) and _ _ _ _ _ _ _ _ _ (_ _ _ _). DRAM is used in more computers than is SRAM. With few exceptions, RAM is also considered to be _ _ _ _ _ _ _ _ _ _ _ _ _ because any data stored there is lost when the power is turned off. Several _ _ _ _ _ _ _ _ _ _ _ _ _ _ _ _ _ _ technologies, such as _ _ _ _ _ _ _ _ _ _ _ _ _ , have emerged, but none has exhibited the qualities necessary for widespread application.

All programs and data must be in primary storage before the CPU can process them. To start WordPerfect, for example, a message from the keyboard is sent to RAM which, in turn, sends it on to the CPU. The CPU processes the message and sends out instructions to the computer system to load the program from secondary storage into RAM in a _ _ _ _ _ _ _ _ _ _ _ _ _ _ _ _ _ _ _ process. This leaves the program intact on the secondary storage media while it is also resident in primary storage. Each program instruction or piece of data loaded are stored in RAM at a specific location or _ _ _ _ _ _ _ .

There is a special type of RAM called read-only memory or ROM. The data and programs stored in ROM are permanent. The only way to change the instructions sent to the computer system from ROM is to change the ROM chip. A special type of read-only memory that allows the user to define the contents of the read-only memory is referred to as _ _ _ _ _ _ _ _ _ _ _ _ _ _ _ _ _ _ -_ _ _ _ _ _ _ _ _ , or _ _ _ _ . A special type of PROM that allows the user to define the contents of the read-only memory, and also to change those contents as necessary, is called _ _ _ _ _ _ _ _ _ _ _ _ . A high-speed holding area for program instructions and data used to increase _ _ _ _ _ _ _ _ _ _ is called _ _ _ _ _ _ _ _ _ _ .

The nucleus of the CPU is the _ _ _ _ _ _ _ _ _ _ _ _ . Its three primary functions are to read and interpret program instructions, direct the operation of internal processor components, and control the flow of programs and data in and out of RAM. A program instruction is decoded and interpreted by the _____ . The control unit also contains several high-speed working storage areas called _____ that can store no more than a few bytes and handle instructions and data at a speed that is faster than that of cache memory. There are several of these areas and they are used for a variety of processing functions. For example, the _____ _____ contains the instruction being executed and the _____ _____ contains the RAM address of the next instruction to be executed.

All computation and logic operations are performed by the _____ ___ _____ _____ . Its _____ contains computational results. Computers solve the most difficult poblems in the world with only seven basic functions. The arithmetic functions are +, -, *, and /, and the logic functions are >, <, and =. If it can be reduced to binary, a computer can be instructed to do something with it.

The computer's control unit, arithmetic and logic unit, memory, and _____ _____ for terminals, printers, scanners, and other system components are all linked by a common electrical ___ . Actually, there are two buses that run simultaneous routes. Source and destination addresses are sent over the _____ ___ to identify a particular location in memory, then the data and instructions are transferred over the ____ ___ to or from that location.

A computer is only capable of working with data and instructions that have been converted into strings of binary digits. Every _____ _____ has a predefined format for each type of instruction. The _____ _____ is the time it takes the CPU to fetch an instruction, decode it, execute it, and place the results in memory. These four functions are divided between the _____ _____ and the _____ ____ . Fetching and decoding an instruction is the _-_____ . The _-____ consists of executing the instruction and placing the results in memory.

Most mainframe and personal computers use ____ architecture. This gives them a wider range of instructions that can be used. This general-purpose capability results in reduced operating speed in certain areas such as graphics applications. When a computer is used for specialized areas such as graphics or mathematical computations, ____ achitecture is often employed to increase throughput.

Another way that designers are looking at to increase throughput is by using multiple processors in the same computer. This is called _____ _____ . By dividing the workload among several special-function processors, the system throughput is increased. If three or four processors can enhance throughput, what could be accomplished with twenty, or even a thousand, processors? Mainframes and supercomputers with thousands of integrated microprocessors are referred to as _____ _____ _____ , (___). These super-fast supercomputers will have sufficient computing capacity to attack applications that have been beyond that of computers with traditional architectures.

2-4

We describe computers or processors in terms of word length, speed, and the capacity of their associated RAM. A _____ is the number of bits that are handled as a unit by a particular computer system. These can be 8, 16, 32, or 64 bits in length, depending on the computer system and system component involved. How a computer's speed is rated depends on the type of computer you are dealing with. Personal computers use a crystal oscillator to pace the execution of instructions within its CPU. The frequency of oscillation of the oscillator, measured in _____ or ___ is, therefore, the speed of a personal computer. CPU speed alone does not tell you if one PC is faster than another, however. It takes both speed and word length to determine that. The processing speed of today's workstations, minis, and mainframes is often measured in _____ , or millions of instructions per second, and supercomputer speed is measured in _____ , or floating point operations per second. State-of-the-art supercomputers are even measured in _____ .

Another important computer measurement is its RAM capacity, or the maximum number of bytes that can be stored in a computer's primary storage. The RAM capacity of most computers is rated in _____ (__) and _____ (__). Some high-end mainframes and supercomputers have over 1000 MB of RAM, and their RAM capacities are stated as

_ _ _ _ _ _ _ _ _   (_ _). It's only a matter of time before we state RAM in terms of
_ _ _ _ _ _ _ _ _   (_ _), about one trillion bytes. Occasionally you will see memory capacities of
some devices and individual chips stated in terms of _ _ _ _ _ _ _ _   (_ _) and _ _ _ _ _ _ _ _
(_ _). Note the difference, especially in the abbreviations.

2-5

    The _ _ _ _ _ _ _ _ _ _ _ _ _ _ _ is a product of the microminiaturization of electronic
circuitry; it is literally a "computer on a chip." Chips are mounted onto a _ _ _ _ _ _ _ that is used to
mount these components onto a _ _ _ _ _ _ _ _ _ _ _ , also called a _ _ _ _ _ _ _ _ _ _ _ . The
Motorola 68K family of microprocessors (68000, 68020, and 68060) have been the processors used in
the Apple computers. However, Apple and others are adopting the new _ _ _ _ _ _ _ technology. The
PowerPC family developed by an alliance of Motorola, Apple, and IBM includes the PowerPC 601, the
PowerPC 603, the PowerPC 604, and the PowerPC 620. The first three are designed for use in PCs, and
the PowerPC 620 is designed for use with everything from high-end workstations to supercomputers. A
major advantage of the PowerPC is that it can run all major industry-standard _ _ _ _ _ _ _ _ _ such as
Apple's System 7 and Microsoft Windows. The Intel 8086 is considered the base technology for all
microprocessors used in IBM-PC compatible and PS/2 series computers. IBM-PC compatible computers
use microprocessors based on the Intel family (8086,8088, 80286, 80386, 80486, and _ _ _ _ _ _ _) of
microprocessors. Intel's successor to the Pentium, called the _ _ , is being installed in high-end
workstations and may someday be the standard for PCs. The Pentium and PowerPC processors are
competing with each other head on. It will be interesting to see if the RISC-based PowerPC can gain
enough acceptance to make significant inroads on Intel's market.

    The computer and its components are also called the computer system configuration.
Attachment of peripheral devices to a computer is possible if the computer uses open architecture. These
attachments are usually made with a cable attached to a receptacle called a _ _ _ _ . There are basically
two types of ports, the _ _ _ _ _ _ _ _ _ _ _ and the _ _ _ _ _ _ _ _ _ _ _ . Connections to these
ports are usually made with either a 9-pin or 25-pin _ _ - _ _ _ connector for serial ports, or a 25-pin
RS-232C connector or _ _ _ _ _ _ _ _ _ _ _ _ _ _ _ _ _ _ for parallel ports.

    Many optional functions are available for microcomputers in the form of _ _ _ _ _ _ _ _ _
_ _ _ _ _ _ which are plugged into _ _ _ _ _ _ _ _ _ _ _ _ _ _ . The optional functions available
with expansion boards or _ _ _ _ _ _ _ _ _ _ _ _ _ _ , as they are alternatives to ISA. ISA can exist
along side innovative new ways to attach peripheral devices and special function expansion boards such
as _ _ _ _ _ _ _ _ technology that transfers data at the processor speeds. The _ _ _ _ _ _ _ _
_ _ _ from Intel Corporation and the Video Electronics Standards Association's (VESA) _ _ - _ _ _
have emerged as alternatives to the expensive MCA and EISA architectures. Another alternative, the
_ _ _ _ _ _ _ (pronounced as "scuzzy" bus), provides for up to seven SCSI (Small Computer System
Interface) peripheral devices to be daisy-chained to a SCSI adapter (an expansion card). This means that
the devices are connected along a single cable with multiple SCSI connectors.

    The expansion slots associated with the expansion buses let you enhance processor functionality
by adding expansion boards. A few examples of these enhancements include the expansion of the
computer's primary memory; a telephone communications device called a _ _ _ _ _ ; a device used to
transfer hard copy images through communications lines called a _ _ _ _ _ _ _ _ (to emulate a
_ _ _ machine); an accelerator used to increase system throughput; and many more. Often, two or
more optional functions can be purchased on a _ _ _ _ _ _ _ _ _ _ _ _ _ _ _ - _ _ _ _ _ _ _ .

    The _ _ _ _ _ _ _ _ _ _ , sometimes called _ _ _ _ _ _ , emerged a few years ago as a
credit-card-sized memory module. PC cards offer supplementary nonvolatile memory and many add-on
board capabilities, including fax modems, network interface adapters, hard disks, and sound. Virtually all
portable computers manufactured today have one or more PCMCIA slots.

PRACTICE TEST

Multiple Choice *Circle the most appropriate answer.*

1. Which of the following is not directly associated with the central processing unit?
    a. control unit
    b. arithmetic and logic unit
    c. accumulator
    d. motor cycle

2. The encoding system used primarily on micros and in data communications is called
    a. ASCII.
    b. EBCDIC.
    c. ANSI.
    d. both EBCDIC and ASCII-8.

3. Which of the following is a proper binary number?
    a. 102101
    b. 1010101
    c. 22101012
    d. B11

4. The raw material from which information is derived is
    a. primary storage.
    b. secondary storage.
    c. data.
    d. PROM.

5. The largest word length available in a microcomputer is
    a. 32 bits.
    b. 128 bits.
    c. 16 bits.
    d. 64 bits.

6. The function of the arithmetic and logic unit is to
    a. perform all computations and all logic operations.
    b. read and interpret program instructions .
    c. direct the operation of internal processor components.
    d. control the flow of programs and data in and out of primary storage.

7. Data are moved from secondary storage into RAM by a
    a. destructive read process.
    b. flash addressing process.
    c. nondestructive read process.
    d. SIMMs process.

8. MIPS stands for
    a. memory-intensive primary storage.
    b. megabytes in processor system.
    c. multidrop information processors.
    d. millions of instructions per second.

9. Which of the following is never included as part of the circuitry on a motherboard?
    a. memory chips
    b. miniature video monitor
    c. microprocessor
    d. circuitry for handling I/O signals

10. The central processing unit in a computer processes
    a. analog signals.   c. digital signals.
    b. alpha signals.   d. SRAM signals.

11. A microcomputer configuration that links expansion boards directly to the system's common bus is referred to as
    a. EISA bus
    b. SCSI bus
    c. VL-bus
    d. ISA bus
12. A Centronics connector is normally used with a
    a. serial port.
    b. parallel port.
    c. SCSI port.
    d. RS-232C port.

True - False *Circle T for true and F for false.*

13. T F A byte is made up of bits.
14. T F To evaluate the processing capability of a micro, consider both the processor speed and word length.
15. T F RAM, ROM, PROM, and flash memory are all examples of secondary storage media.
16. T F Programs and data must be transferred to primary storage before programs can be executed or data can be processed.
17. T F CISC chips, as opposed to RISC chips, are especially appropriate for specialized workstation-based applications.
18. T F Every computer has a machine cycle.
19. T F Primary and secondary storage capacities are usually stated in terms of picoseconds and megabytes.
20. T F Letters and decimal numbers are represented in a computer system by coded combinations of bits.
21. T F Both upper case "K" and the lower case "k" have the same ASCII bit configuration.
22. T F The term ASCII stands for American Standard Code for Integrated Interchange.
23. T F The binary digits are commonly represented by the numbers 1 and 2.
24. T F The characteristics of CMOS memory make it superior to bubble memory when used with industrial robots.
25. T F In semiconductor primary storage, the data are lost when the current is turned off or interrupted.
26. T F RAM is a form of temporary data storage.
27. T F A system board is mounted in a carrier and then inserted into a micro.
28. T F Parallel ports are available in 9-pin and 36-pin versions.
29. T F Keyboards, printers, and monitors are also called peripheral devices.
30. T F The microcomputer is also called a "computer on a chip."

Matching

Match the following terms with the appropriate definition or characteristic by placing the letter of the matching definition or characteristic in the blank.

31. _____ primary storage

32. _____ throughput

33. _____ bit

34. _____ encoding system

35. _____ alpha

36. _____ numeric

37. _____ Mb

38. _____ central processing unit

39. _____ megabyte

40. _____ arithmetic and logic unit

41. _____ RS-232C

42. _____ massively parallel processing

(a) One million bytes

(b) Rules for combining bits to represent letters, numbers, and special characters

(c) Houses the control unit and the arithmetic and logic unit

(d) Data are stored here temporarily during processing

(e) A type of connector used to connect peripheral devices with serial and parallel ports on a computer.

(f) Part of the CPU that performs computations and comparisons

(g) Short for binary digit

(h) An approach to the design of computer systems that involves the integration of thousands of microprocessors within a single computer.

(i) Numbers (e.g., 1, 4, 7)

(j) Abbreviation for megabit

(k) The rate at which work can be performed by a computer system

(l) Letters (e.g., A, G, m, q)

Answers to Practice Test **1** d, **2** a, **3** b, **4** c, **5** d, **6** a, **7** a, **8** a, **9** d, **10** b, **11** c, **12** b, **13** t, **14** t, **15** f, **16** t, **17** f, **18** t, **19** f, **20** t, **21** f, **22** t, **23** f, **24** f, **25** t, **26** t, **27** f, **28** f, **29** t, **30** f, **31** d, **32** k, **33** g, **34** b, **35** l, **36** i, **37** j, **38** c, **39** a, **40** f, **41** e, **42** h.

CHAPTER CHECKUP

NAME		DATE	CHAPTER 2
COURSE	SECTION	INSTRUCTOR	

1. From a user's perspective, what is the difference between temporary and permanent storage of data in a computer system? *A good way to remember the difference between temporary (or primary) storage and permanent (or secondary) storage is to visualize turning the electrical power off to the computer.*

2. What is the relationship between data and secondary storage? *See section 2-1 and section 2-2 of the text.*

3. What is the similarity between a bit and a light switch? *See section 2-1 and section 2-2 of the text.*

4. Why is the binary numbering system especially appropriate for the storage of data inside a computer? *What is the purpose of a light switch? See section 2-1 of the text.*

5. What is an encoding system? Give an example of an encoding system. *See section 2-2 of the text.*

6. Identify each of the following characters as alpha, numeric, or special characters. *See section 2-2 of the text.*

D

*

8

P

1

Z

7. Use Figure 2-4 in the text to decode the following ASCII message: *Be sure to read the caption to the figure. See section 2-2 of the text.*

1000101	1101110	1100011	1101111	1100100	1101001	1101110	1100111
0100000	1010011	1111001	1110011	1110100	1100101	1101101	

8. "CPU" is an abbreviation for what? *See section 2-3 of the text.*

9. What are the two fundamental sections of the CPU? *See section 2-3 of the text.*

■

■

10. What is the relationship between PROM and flash memory? *See section 2-3 of the text.*

11. List the three primary functions of the control unit. *One of these functions has to do with instructions.*

■

■

■

12. Identify each of the following properties as either a property of CMOS memory or of bubble memory: *See section 2-3 of the text.*

(a)   not susceptible to environmental fluctuations

(b)   data are lost when electrical current is turned off

(c)   used by most of today's computers for primary storage

(d)   considered a "nonvolatile" technology

(e)   good for use in industrial robots and portable computers.

13. What is the purpose of the arithmetic and logic unit? *See section 2-3 of the text.*

14. Briefly describe the four activities of a machine cycle. *See section 2-3 of the text.*

■

■

■

■

15. Define parallel processing. *See section 2-3 of the text.*

16. Translate the description "50 MHz, 6 Mb, 32-bit micro" into everyday terms. *See section 2-4 of the text.*

17. If your heart beats approximately 105,000 times every day, how fast (in MIPS) must a processor be to execute as many instructions in 1 minute as your heart has beaten since you were born? *For a 30-year old, it's about 20 MIPS.*

18. Briefly describe the difference between a parallel port and a serial port. *These are used to provide most peripheral devices with access to the CPU. Why is communications with one faster than the other?*

19. What hardware components would be included in a typical microcomputer configuration? *The question asks about hardware as opposed to software.*

20.   Compose a multiple-choice, a true/false, and an essay question that you think would be appropriate for a quiz on this chapter.

M/C:

(a)

(b)

(c)

(d)

T/F:

Essay:

GRAPHICAL USER INTERFACE

You have just typed in the command to start WordPerfect and tapped enter. Use arrows to depict the path of this command through the computer hardware components pictured below. Number each arrow in the order in which the command travels.

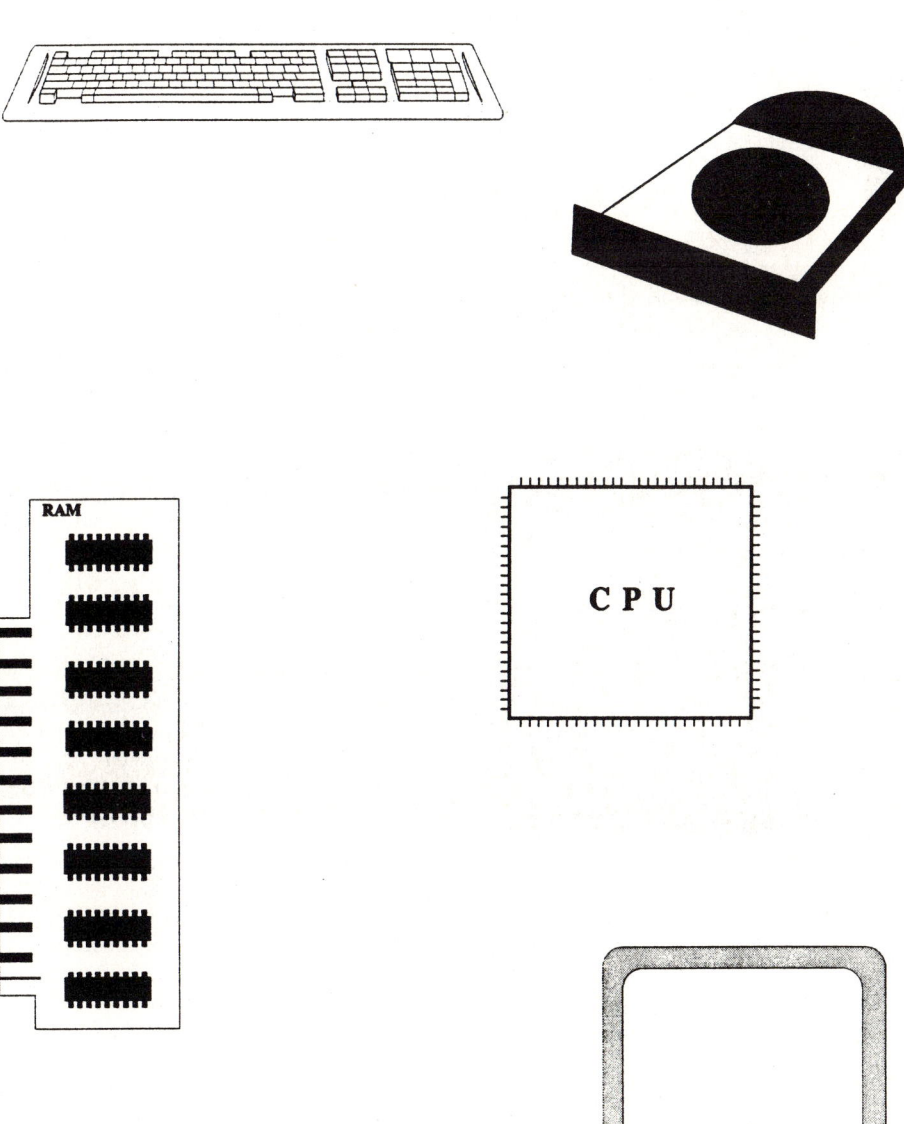

**Chapter 3
Software:
Telling Computers What to Do**

STUDENT LEARNING OBJECTIVES

- To demonstrate an understanding of common system software concepts.
- To detail the purpose and objectives of an operating system.
- To understand the relationship between computers and programming languages.
- To distinguish between several different types of programming languages.
- To describe the capabilities of visual programming languages and natural languages.
- To describe what constitutes a platform.
- To distinguish between common platforms available to microcomputer users.
- To understand the scope of knowledge needed to interact effectively with a personal computer.
- To grasp concepts related to the effective use of computers and software.
- To describe various keyboard, mouse, and data entry conventions.

VOCABULARY STUDY

applications software
background
boot
click
computer virus
cross-platform technologies
default option
dialog box
dimmed
double-click
drag
exit routine
foreground
fourth-generation language
(FOURTH GENERATION
LANGUAGE)
function key
graphical user interface (GUI)
graphics cursor
icon
interoperability
invoke
kernel

keyboard template
macro
macro language
main menu
menu
menu bar
menu tree
mnemonic
MS-DOS
multiplatform environment
multitasking
natural language
object program
object-oriented language
object-oriented programming
(OOP)
operating system
OS/2
parameter
platform
plug-and-play
pop-out menu
pop-up menu

power up
procedure-oriented language
programmer
programming
programming language
pull-down menu
syntax
scrolling
shut down
simultaneous click
software installation
System (Apple operating system)
system check
system prompt
system software
text cursor
user interface
Visual Basic
visual programming
Windows (operating system)
Windows 95
Windows NT
workgroup computing

INTERACTIVE REVIEW

Use the Vocabulary Study terms to fill in the following blanks. You will only use each term once. You may need to insert a plural form of a term or adjust its verb tense. Check your answers with the chapter material and the glossary in your textbook.

3-1

A computer can only do what it's told to do, the way it's told to do it. Without a program, it's just a fancy paperweight. Software is one or more programs that instruct a computer to accomplish a task. The instructions in programs are logically sequenced and assembled through the act of _ use any number of existing _ to write programs for computers.

3-2

When a computer is started up, the _ _ _ _ _ _ _ _ _ _ _ _ _ _ _ takes control of the computer and plays a central role in all interactions with the computer. Virtually all PC operating systems produced today are designed to work along with a user-friendly graphical user interface (GUI). System software is required for _ _ _ _ _ _ _ _ _ _ _ _ _ _ _ _ _ _ _ , such as word processing, tax planning, or computer games, to operate and interact effectively with the hardware components of the computer.

3-3

A computer's _ _ _ _ _ _ _ _ _ _ _ _ _ _ _ _ is responsible for ongoing operation control, input/output control, and file and disk management. One of the operating system programs, often called the _ _ _ _ _ _ , loads other operating system and applications programs to RAM as they are needed. All operating systems are designed with the same basic objectives in mind. However, mainframe and micro operating systems differ markedly in complexity and orientation. Efficient operating systems use _ _ _ _ _ _ _ _ _ _ _ _ to concurrently execute two or more programs. In multitasking, the current or active program runs in the _ _ _ _ _ _ _ _ _ _ while other lower-priority programs run in the _ _ _ _ _ _ _ _ _ _ . Through the 1980s, the most popular microcomputer operating system, _ _ - _ _ _ , was strictly text-based, command-driven software. Command-driven software requires strict adherence to proper _ _ _ _ _ _ when entering commands. In contrast, the _ (_ _ _) uses an integration of text and graphic images on the screen to present command options in the form of an _ _ _ _ for selection with a mouse or other pointing device. All modern operating systems, including the _ _ _ _ _ _ _ _ _ operating system, provide a GUI as an alternative to the cryptic command-driven interface. GUIs have effectively eliminated the need for users to memorize and enter cumbersome commands.

3-4

We create software with programming languages. With programming, the design of a program, or its programming logic, is completed before the program is written. Each programming language has an instruction set with several instructions for input/output, computation, control, assignment, and formatting. In Chapter 2, we learned that all programs are executed in machine language, the computer's native language. Programs written in any other language must be translated into machine language before they can be executed. The difficulty of programming in machine language led to the advent of _ _ _ _ _ _ _ _ _ - _ _ _ _ _ _ _ _ _ _ _ _ _ _ _ _ _ _ beginning in 1955. Procedure-oriented languages require programmers to solve programming problems using traditional programming logic. Examples include COBOL and FORTRAN. In _ _ _ _ _ _ _ - _ (_ _ _), the emphasis is on the object of the action. Objects include fields, procedures, and an identity. Primary benefits of _ _ _ _ _ _ - _ _ _ _ _ _ _ _ _ _ - _ _ _ _ _ _ _ _ _ include increased programmer productivity and clarity of logic. C++ and Smalltalk are two popular examples.

_ _ _ _ _ _ _ - _ (_ _ _) allow the programmer to specify what to do without having to specify how to do it. The features of a 4GL include English-like instructions, limited mathematical manipulation of data, automatic report formatting, sequencing, record

selection by criteria, and they are very easy to use (relatively speaking). _ _ _ _ _ _
_ _ _ _ _ _ _ _ _ _ _ replaces many text-based instructions with symbolic icons. However, even
_ _ _ _ _ _ _ _ _ _ programs have some written instructions.

The term _ _ _ _ _ _ _ _ _ _ _ _ _ _ _ _ _ refers to software that enables computer systems to accept, interpret, and execute instructions in the native language of the end user. With little or no training, end users should be able to use these languages to write their own programs for reports and processing without the assistance of computer programming specialists.

Another form of programming is provided by some applications which allow you to create a _ _ _ _ _ for a sequence of frequently used operations or keystrokes, such as a series of selections from a list of options called a _ _ _ _ . Once created and stored on disk, the user can _ _ _ _ _ _ a macro to perform its task almost any time in the application with only one or two keystrokes. Many applications are distributed with their own _ _ _ _ _ _ _ _ _ _ _ _ _ that allow the user to include conditions and options in their macros along with keystroke replacement. Most macro languages are unique to the application in which they are distributed. A little bit of programming ability can go a long way. Automation of time consuming, routine computer activities with even crude macros and programs can save hours every week, time that can be used more productively.

3-5

A _ _ _ _ _ _ _ _ _ defines a standard for which software packages are developed. A platform is defined by the processor and operating system with which it is used. Software created to run on one platform is not usually compatible with any other platform. While most computer systems can only run under one platform, some are able to emulate other platforms. Programs running in emulation mode run more slowly than if run on the real thing. Before choosing a platform, consider the availability of appropriate commercial applications software for the platform and the compatibility of platform with existing hardware, software, and expertise. Platforms for PCs can be either for single-user or multiuser environments. The most popular single user platforms are MS-DOS, Windows95, and System. MS-DOS still remains extremely popular among users with micros that are functionally compatible with the 1984 IBM PC-AT architecture. Many PC users run Microsoft's _ _ _ _ _ _ _ within MS-DOS. The advantages of Windows over MS-DOS include increased user-friendliness, the ability to run multiple programs simultaneously, the ability to work with large files, and the ability to pass information between applications. A disadvantage is that programs run under Windows tend to run slower than if they were run under MS-DOS without Windows. Windows95 replaces both MS-DOS and the old Windows with a single platform. Windows95 promises to reduce or eliminate the problems and inefficiencies of the old MS-DOS/Windows combination. Windows 95 offers the _ _ _ _ - _ _ _ - _ _ _ _ capability which is supposed to make it easier to add peripherals to a computer system.

The Apple Macintosh family of microcomputers and _ _ _ _ _ _ _ , its operating system, define another major platform that accounts for about 10 percent of the PCs. The Macintosh platform includes multitasking, a GUI, virtual memory, the ability to emulate the MS-DOS and MS-DOS/Windows platforms and the ability to communicate with and share files with other Macintosh computers on a network. In addition to Microsoft and Apple, IBM has developed _ _ / _ which has experienced a small degree of acceptance among IBM compatible users.

PC-level multiuser platforms are either UNIX-based or designed to support _ _ _ _ _ _ _ _ _ _ _ _ _ _ _ _ _ _ _ . UNIX is available with PC-compatible, Macintosh, and PowerPC-based PCs. Many of the popular PC software packages have been retrofitted to run under UNIX. The most visible workgroup platforms are Windows95 and _ _ _ _ _ _ _ _ _ _ . _ _ _ _ _ _ _ _ _ _ is developed to run under workgroup platforms. The selection of a platform for corporate computing can be very complex, even for seasoned computer professionals, and represents a sizable investment on the part of the organization. Eventually, advancing technology forces the organization to choose between continuing with their existing platform or upgrading to another, which may or may not be compatible with the existing one. A company must either standardize entirely on one platform or invest in technology to achieve _ _ _ _ _ _ _ _ _ _ _ _ _ _ _ _ _ _ necessary to share applications and exchange information across platforms in a _ . Enabling technologies that allow communication and the sharing of resources between different platforms are called _ _ _ _ _ -

_ _ _ _ _ _ _ _ _ _ _ _ _ _ _ _ _ _ _ _ _ . Whenever possible, companies try to minimize the number of platforms represented in the company. The fewer the number of platforms, the easier and cheaper it is to install and maintain cross-platform technologies.

3-6

In order for you to be able to effectively interact with computer systems, you need to have a working knowledge of general software concepts, the operation and use of the hardware over which you have control, the function and use of the computer's operating system and/or its graphical user interface (GUI), and the specific applications programs you are using.

_ _ _ _ _ _ _ _ _ _ _ _ _ _ _ _ _ _ _ _ is a two-step process. The first is to install the software onto the computer system by simply following the instructions that came with the package. Different software packages use different procedures. Second, set the predefined system settings, or _ _ _ _ _ _ _ _ _ _ _ _ _ _ as they are called, in the software to conform with the configuration of your computer system. When you find yourself in need of a more detailed explanation or instructions on how to proceed, most software packages provide you with a _ _ _ _ _ _ _ _ _ _ _ that displays context-sensitive explanations.

A PC computing session begins with turning the computer on. When you _ _ _ _ _ _ _ _ a computer system, you also _ _ _ _ the system which involves a whole sequence of automatically executed events. A program permanently stored in read-only memory (ROM) is executed and performs a _ _ _ _ _ _ _ _ _ _ _ and loads the operating system from permanent magnetic storage into RAM. The operating system executes predefined user instructions, then requests instructions from the user by presenting a _ _ _ _ _ _ _ _ _ _ _ _ _ _ , an icon, or a menu. Upon ending a PC computing session, you do not simply flip the computer switch to off. You must _ _ _ _ _ _ _ _ in an orderly manner. This involves executing an _ _ _ _ _ _ _ _ _ _ _ _ for all active applications programs prior to shutting off the power.

With very few exceptions, the primary input and control device for computer systems is the keyboard. Besides the standard typewriter keyboard layout, most keyboards have _ _ _ _ _ _ _ _ _ _ _ _ _ that trigger the execution of software such as calling up a displayed list of user options commonly referred to as a menu. Because different software packages assign different functions to these keys, the user is often provided with a _ _ _ _ _ _ _ _ _ _ _ _ _ _ _ _ _ to help keep track of which keys do what. You will usually find a numeric key pad, which looks similar to the keys on a basic calculator, and cursor-control keys, which are used to control the movement of the _ _ _ _ _ _ _ _ _ _ . _ _ _ _ _ _ _ _ _ _ allows the user to move about within a document. In addition, several other keys are found on a computer keyboard. How many of these special function keys can you list and describe?

Point and draw devices are becoming very popular input devices with the increased use of GUIs. The most popular of these devices is the mouse. The mouse is used to move the _ _ _ _ _ _ _ _ _ _ _ _ _ _ around the monitor screen. Most mice and other point-and-draw devices have at least two buttons. To make a selection or execute a command, you usually tap, or _ _ _ _ _ _ , the left button. The function of the right button varies between software packages. A _ _ _ _ _ _ _ - _ _ _ _ _ , which is tapping a button twice in rapid succession, gives each button a different meaning. Some software packages permit a _ _ _ _ _ _ _ _ _ _ _ _ _ _ _ _ _ _ _ _ _ _ , or tapping both buttons simultaneously, to give the mouse added functionality. Press and hold a button to _ _ _ _ the graphics cursor across the screen.

Software designers continue to create new and more efficient ways for us to issue commands and initiate operations. These include a variety of menus and button bars. Menus are often arranged in hierarchies called _ _ _ _ _ _ _ _ _ _ _ . The first menu in the hierarchy is called the _ _ _ _ _ _ _ _ _ . A _ _ _ _ _ _ _ menu selection means that it is disabled or unavailable. Menus are presented in five basic formats. The main menu is frequently presented as a _ _ _ _ _ _ _ in the _ _ _ _ _ _ _ _ _ _ _ portion of the display. Selection from a menu bar at the top of the screen usually results in the display of a subordinate menu bar or a _ _ _ _ - _ _ _ _ _ _ _ _ _ . The _ _ _ - _ _ _ _ _ _ is superimposed on the current screen in a window. Context-sensitive pop-up menus are often available by clicking the right mouse button. The _ _ _ - _ _ _ _ _ _ is displayed next to the menu option selected in a higher level of the menu tree. The floating menu floats over the work area until you no longer need it. There are three ways to select an item from a menu. Use the left/right or up/down arrow keys to highlight the desired menu option and tap Enter. From the keyboard, enter the _ _ _ _ _ _ _ _ of the desired item. Use the mouse (or other point and draw device) to point and click. Eventually you will be asked to enter the specifications or variables, called _ _ _ _ _ _ _ _ _ , before the current command can be executed. These are normally entered and revised in a _ _ _ _ _ _ _ _ _ .

In addition to menus, _ _ _ _ _ _ _ _ _ _ contain a group of rectangular graphics that represent a menu option or a command. To execute a particular command, simply click on the button. The graphics on the buttons are designed to represent actions of the command. Most applications allow you to customize your button bars to meet your processing needs.

PRACTICE TEST

Multiple Choice *Circle the best answer.*

1. The interface between the user and applications programs is provided by
   a. a CRT.
   b. either the computer's operating system or a GUI.
   c. a computer hardware item called TRON.
   d. a computer program called WYSIWYG.

2. An objective not associated with that of an operating system is
   a. optimizing the use of system resources.
   b. minimizing throughput.
   c. minimizing turnaround time.
   d. facilitating communication between the system and users.

3. General ledger software falls under which category of software?
   a. general-purpose
   b. human resource
   c. applications
   d. systems

4. Windows95 is designed to replace which of the following combinations?
   a. Windows NT and MS-DOS
   b. Windows and UNIX
   c. Windows and MS-DOS
   d. Windows and OS/2

5. The Macintosh platform uses
   a. the OS/2 operating system.
   b. the Intel family of microprocessors.
   c. NuBus 32-bit architecture.
   d. EISA 32-bit architecture.

6. Which term is not associated with using menus?
   a. pop-up
   b. pull-apart
   c. pull-down
   d. window

7. Instructions that can alter the sequence of a program's execution are
   a. input/output instructions.
   b. computation instructions.
   c. data transfer and assignment instructions.
   d. control instructions.

8. Which of the following is not considered a function of the PC operating system?
  a. word processing
  b. controls the ongoing operations of the computer system
  c. handles file and disk management tasks
  d. provides input/output controls

9. The operating system program, often called the kernel,
  a. loads other system programs to primary storage as they are needed.
  b. compiles source programs.
  c. keeps score and gauges time for computer games.
  d. eliminates the need for a user interface.

10. Which of the following is a multiuser operating system?
  a. UNIX
  b. OS/2
  c. MS-DOS
  d. PC-DOS

11. A programming tool provided by some applications programs that can be created to replace repetitive keystrokes and commands is called a
  a. marker.
  b. macro.
  c. master.
  d. marco.

12. If a Help command is context sensitive,
  a. it uses icons.
  b. it is divided into window panes.
  c. it is in a CUA format.
  d. the explanation relates to what you were doing when you issued the command.

True - False *Circle T for true and F for false.*

13. T F Spreadsheet software would be considered applications software.
14. T F MS-DOS and UNIX are examples of applications software.
15. T F A keyboard template provides a visual cue to what function keys do for a particular software package.
16. T F The term platform refers to the desk on which a PC rests.
17. T F Parameters are user-defined variables that are set prior to entering commands for an application.
18. T F Clicks, also called icons, are used to help software to be more user friendly.
19. T F In a computer system, the hardware and software are under the control of the operating system.
20. T F Another name for cursor control keys is function keys.
21. T F The programming language common to all computers at the lowest level is mnemonics language.
22. T F Programmers code in high-level programming languages by writing instructions as a series of binary digits.
23. T F Most computers can directly execute many computer languages without having to translate them into another form or code.
24. T F Parameters are normally entered and revised in a dialogue box.
25. T F Macros are similar to tutorials and are used to help new users learn about integrated software packages.
26. T F The pop-out menu is displayed next to the menu option selected in a higher-level pull-down or pop-up menu.
27. T F A dimmed menu option indicates a selection is available.

28.   T F   Software applications developed specifically to run under Windows must follow the Windows Common User Access.

29.   T F   Fourth-generation languages enable managers to create their own applications systems.

30.   T F   Windows95 can replace both Windows and Macintosh System.

Matching *Match the following terms with the appropriate definition or characteristic by placing the letter of the matching definition or characteristic in the blank.*

31. _____ applications software

32. _____ invoke

33. _____ text cursor

34. _____ CUA

35. _____ system check

36. _____ kernel

37. _____ UNIX

38. _____ software

39. _____ graphics cursor

40. _____ multitasking

41. _____ NuBus

42. _____ dialog box

(a) A general term used to refer to programs collectively

(b) An internal verification of the operational capabilities of a computer

(c) Operating system used on both mainframes and multiuser micros

(d) The concurrent execution of more than one program at a time

(e) A term used to describe the execution of a macro in an applications program.

(f) Type of window used to display parameter options

(g) Apple Computer's state-of-the-art architecture

(h) On screen symbol that can be moved by a light pen, joystick, or mouse to initiate action or to draw

(i) Programs designed and written to perform specific personal, business, or scientific processing tasks

(j) Conventions that all Windows applications must adhere to

(k) Indicates the location of the next keyed-in character on the screen

(l) loads other operating system and applications programs to RAM as they are needed

Answers to Practice Test **1** b, **2** b, **3** c, **4** c, **5** c, **6** b, **7** d, **8** a, **9** a, **10** a, **11** b, **12** d, **13** t, **14** f, **15** t, **16** f, **17** t, **18** f, **19** t, **20** f, **21** f, **22** f, **23** f, **24** t, **25** f, **26** t, **27** f, **28** t, **29** t, **30** f, **31** i, **32** e, **33** f, **34** j, **35** b, **36** l, **37** c, **38** a, **39** h, **40** g, **41** d, **42** f.

CHAPTER CHECKUP

NAME		DATE	CHAPTER 3
COURSE	SECTION	INSTRUCTOR	

1. How do function keys save time? *See section 3-6 of the text.*

2. What are the major design objectives for an operating system? *On a multiuser computer system, users compete for the physical resources of the computer and also share data and programs. The operating system makes this sharing and competition for resources fair by allocating resources according to rules called system parameters. See section 3-3 of the text.*

3. Why does the operating system need a vehicle by which to interact with a human operator? *See section 3-3 of the text.*

4. What is the difference between the foreground and background part of RAM? *See section 3-3 of the text.*

5. How is the term context-sensitive related to the Help command in most software packages? *See section 3-6 of the text.*

6. What defines a platform? *See section 3-1 of the text.*

7. Give two reasons why the MS-DOS and Windows platforms have dominated the PC arena during recent years. *See section 3-5 of the text.*

■

■

8. Describe two advantages (over DOS) of using Microsoft's Windows software. *There are many different reasons and most of them have to do with the user interface.*

■

■

9. Computer programs often use a display structure called a dialog box. What is a dialog box and how might you use it? *These often appear when you initially set up a new program to operate within your computer's configuration.*

10. Why are computer programs needed? *See section 3-1 of the text.*

11. What is the difference between a text cursor and a graphics cursor? *See section 3-6 of the text.*

12. Although relatively few programmers code programs in machine language, machine language is present on all computer systems. Why? *It has to do with execution. See section 3-4 of the text.*

13. List four areas with which you should be familiar when interacting with a personal computer. *See section 3-6 of the text.*

■

■

■

■

14. Name one advantage and one disadvantage of 4GLs. *See section 3-4 of the text.*

■

■

15. How have fourth-generation languages changed the way management personnel access their company's information resource? How have fourth-generation languages changed the programmer's role? *See section 3-4 of the text.*

16. Describe the differences between procedure-oriented computer languages and object-oriented computer languages. *See section 3-4 of the text.*

17. What is a macro? *Combined keystrokes is part of it. See section 3-4 of the text.*

18. Describe the basic concepts of object-oriented computer programming. *See section 3-4 of the text.*

19. Describe each of the following in terms of appearance and user interaction: *These function in a hierarchy. A selection from one often leads down to another until the function you desire is displayed. See section 3-6 of the text.*

(a) menu bar

(b) pull-down menu

(c) pop-up menu

(d) pop-out menu.

20. Compose a multiple-choice, a true/false, and an essay question that you think would be appropriate for a quiz on this chapter.

M/C:
(a)
(b)
(c)
(d)
T/F:
Essay:

GRAPHICAL USER INTERFACE

Choose the operating system or systems (shown in the five disks) that would be appropriate for each of the computer systems pictured below. The options are: 1) Windows95; 2) Macintosh System; 3) OS/2; 4) Windows NT; and 5) UNIX. Note that C and E are PC compatibles and D is a Macintosh.

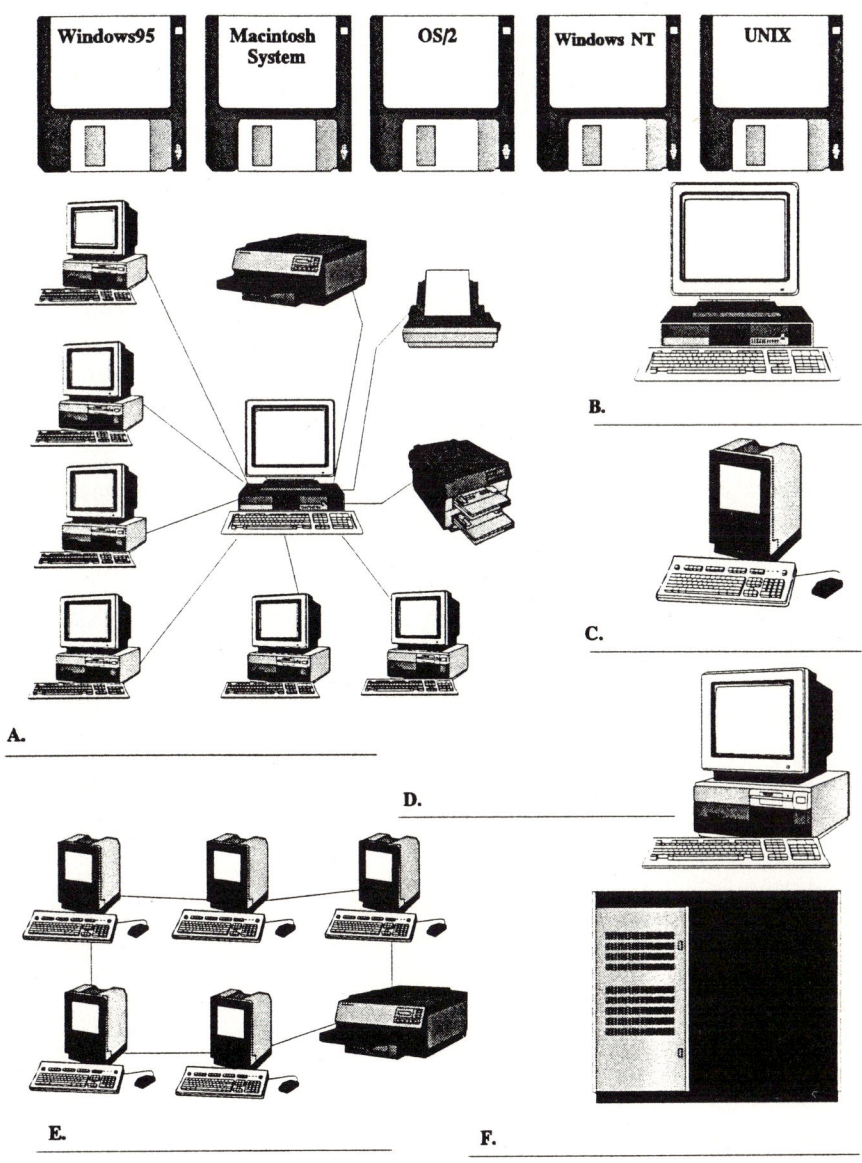

Chapter 4
Storing and Retrieving
Information: Disks and Tape
Backup Units

STUDENT LEARNING OBJECTIVES

- To distinguish between primary and secondary storage.
- To describe how data are stored and retrieved in computer systems.
- To demonstrate an understanding of the fundamental principles of sequential and random access.
- To distinguish between secondary storage devices and secondary storage media.
- To describe the principles of operation, methods of data storage, and use of magnetic disk and magnetic tape drives.
- To know types and sources of computer virus.
- To describe procedures for backing up disk files to data cartridge or diskette.
- To discuss the applications and use of optical laser disk storage.

VOCABULARY STUDY

access arm
access time
ASCII file
audio file
CD production station
CD writer
compact disk-recordable (CD-R)
cylinder
data cartridge
data file
data transfer rate
direct-access storage device
(DASD)
disk address
disk caching
disk density
diskette
document file
executable program file

export
file
file allocation table (FAT)
file compression
fixed magnetic disk
floppy disk
floptical disk drive
formatted
graphics file
import
interchangeable magnetic disk
jukeboxes
magnetic disk drive
magnetic tape cartridge
magnetic tape drive
magneto-optical technology
optical laser disk
random processing

read/write head
rewritable optical disk
secondary storage
sector
sector organization
sequential processing
serial representation
serpentine
source program file
spreadsheet file
tape backup unit (TBU)
track
tracks per inch (TPI)
video file
WORM disk
WORM disk cartridge

INTERACTIVE REVIEW

Use the terms in the Vocabulary Study to fill in the following blanks. You will only use each term once. You may need to insert a plural form of a term or adjust its verb tense. Check your answers with the chapter material and the glossary in your textbook.

4-1

Applications are stored permanently for periodic retrieval in relatively inexpensive
_ _ _ _ _ _ _ _ _ _ _ _ _ _ _ _ _ . Secondary storage systems that dominate today's computer systems
are _ _ _ _ _ _ _ _ _ _ _ _ _ _ _ _ _ _ , _ _ _ _ _ _ _ _ _ _ _ _ _ _ _ _ _ _ , and _ _ _ _ _ _ _ _
_ _ _ _ _ _ _ _ _ . The _ _ _ _ _ is the foundation of permanent storage on a computer system. An _ _ _ _ _
_ _ _ _ is a text-only file that can be read or created by any word processing program or text editor. A
_ _ _ _ _ _ _ _ contains data organized into records. A word processing or desktop publishing
_ _ _ _ _ _ _ _ _ _ _ _ contains integrated text and images. A _ _ _ _ _ _ _ _ _ _ _ _ _ _ _
contains rows and columns of data. A _ _ _ _ _ _ _ _ _ _ _ _ _ _ _ _ _ _ contains high-level
instructions to the computer. An _ contains executable
machine language code. A _ _ _ _ _ _ _ _ _ _ _ _ contains digitized images. An _ _ _ _ _ _ _ _ _ _
contains digitized sound. A _ _ _ _ _ _ _ _ _ contains digitized video frames that when played
rapidly, produce motion video. In the MS-DOS/Windows environment, the name of a file includes a
filename of one to eight characters and an optional extension of up to three characters. The filename and
extension are separated by a period (.). The extension identifies files with a certain application.
Everything we do on a computer has to do with a file and, therefore, "secondary storage. We create,
name, save, copy, move, delete, retrieve, update, display, print, play, execute, download, upload, and
export/import, compress, and protect files. When we _ _ _ _ _ _ _ a file, we convert it from its foreign
format to a format that is compatible with the current program. When we _ _ _ _ _ _ _ a file, we
convert a file in the current program to a format needed by another program. The process of _ _ _ _
_ _ _ _ _ _ _ _ _ replaces repeated data patterns in a file with a brief descriptor.

4-2

Operationally, the magnetic tape is the same as the one in home and automobile audiotape
decks. The magnetic disk can be compared to a compact disk (CD). Magnetic tape can be used for
sequential access only. While magnetic disk drives provide a computer system with _ _ _ _ _ _ - and
_ _ _ _ _ _ _ _ _ _ _ - _ _ _ _ _ _ _ _ _ _ capabilities.

4-3

Magnetic disk storage is the overwhelming choice of computer users, whether on micros,
workstations, or supercomputers. A variety of magnetic disk drives (the hardware device) and magnetic
disks (the media) are manufactured for different business requirements. _ _ _ _ _ _ _ _ _ _ _ _ _ _ _ _
_ _ _ _ _ _ _ _ _ _ _ can be stored off-line and loaded to the magnetic disk drives as they are
needed. _ _ _ _ _ _ _ _ _ _ _ _ _ _ _ _ _ _ _ are permanently installed, or fixed. Today's integrated
software and databases require all data and programs to be on-line at all times. Virtually all PCs sold
today are configured with at least one hard disk drive and one interchangeable disk drive.
Interchangeable magnetic disks for PCs are called _ _ _ _ _ _ _ _ _ _ . They come in two sizes, the
5¼-inch _ _ _ _ _ _ _ _ _ , and the 3½-inch diskette. Floppies have a flexible protective jacket and
are rated by _ _ _ _ _ _ _ _ _ _ and number of recording sides. Today, there are only two types of
floppy drives available for PCs, the 360-KB DS/DD and the 1.2-MB DS/HD. The 3½-inch diskette has
a rigid protective cover and is primarily available in 720-KB DS/DD and 1.44-MB DS/HD capacities.
Currently there are 3½-inch drives available that can store 2.88-MB on a disk. There is also a
_ _ _ _ _ _ _ _ _ _ _ _ _ _ _ _ _ _ that can read and write up to 28-MB diskettes or use the
standard 3½-inch diskettes.

The 1- to 5¼-inch hard disks have storage capacities that range from about 40 MB (megabytes)
to 3 GB (gigabytes). Data are stored in a hard disk drive on all recording surfaces. The

_ _ _ _ _ / _ _ _ _ _ _ _ _ _ _ on a hard disk are mounted on _ _ _ _ _ _ _ _ _ _ that float over (or under) the spinning recording surfaces at extremely close tolerances. Normally, hard disk drives are permanently installed in the computer cabinet, but there are interchangeable hard disks available, too.

Data are stored on disks in _ _ _ _ _ _ using serial representation. The spacing of tracks on a magnetic disk is measured in _ _ _ _ _ _ _ _ _ _ _ _ _ _ or _ _ _ . The recording density is measured in bits per inch (not bytes). In _ _ _ _ _ _ _ _ _ _ _ _ _ _ _ _ _ _ _ , the recording surface is divided into pie-shaped _ _ _ _ _ _ _ _ , and each is given a unique number. A _ _ _ _ _ _ _ _ _ _ is made up of a track number and a sector number. In multiple-disk hard disk drives, a _ _ _ _ _ _ _ _ _ consists of the same numbered track on all disks in the drive. An address for this type of drive would normally consist of a cylinder number, a recording surface number, and a sector number.

Before the disk can be used, it must be _ _ _ _ _ _ _ _ _ _ . The formatting procedure causes the disk to be initialized with a recording format for your operating system by creating sectors and tracks into which data are stored, and setting up an area for the _ _ _ _ _ _ _ _ _ _ _ _ _ _ _ _ _ (_ _ _). The file allocation table tells the system where to find the files and directories you eventually store on the disk, that is, what sector and track. _ _ _ _ _ _ _ _ _ _ is the interval between the instant a computer makes a request for transfer of data from a disk-storage device to RAM and the instant this operation is completed. The _ _ _ _ _ _ _ _ _ _ _ _ _ _ _ is the rate at which data are read from (written to) secondary storage to (from) RAM.

_ _ _ _ _ _ _ _ _ _ _ places programs and data that are likely to be called into RAM for processing from a disk into an area of RAM that simulates disk storage. Hard disk drives for mainframes are very similar to those for PCs except that mainframe drives are generally much bigger and store a lot more data. A single diskette can represent weeks or even months of hard work. Therefore it is important to remember the dos and don'ts for handling interchangeable disks.

_ _ _ _ _ _ _ - _ (_ _ _ _ _), such as magnetic disk, are the prerequisites for all information systems where the data must be on-line and accessed directly. The trend in mainframe drives is to permanently installed drives, although you may occasionally run onto a disk cartridge or disk pack in an older computer system. The biggest threat to data on a hard disk is a computer virus. There are several different types of computer viruses and they most commonly enter a computer system from the public electronic bulletin boards, diskettes used to install programs or share data with other computer systems, and from computer networks. A computer virus can destroy all the data and programs on a computer system and even destroy hardware components.

4-4

Magnetic tape and magnetic disk are the two most popular forms of secondary storage because they are reliable, inexpensive, and have both read and write capability. Magnetic tape can only be used for sequential processing. A record cannot be copied from a tape, processed, and rewritten to the same tape without rewriting the entire tape. Magnetic tape systems today are used for backup, archiving files, and for transporting files between computers. The _ , which is also called a _ _ _ _ _ _ _ _ _ _ _ _ _ , is self-contained and is inserted into and removed from the tape drive in much the same way you would load or remove a videotape from a VCR. When on-line, or operating, the tape passes under the read/write head and data are either transmitted from the tape to primary storage for processing or data are transmitted from RAM to the tape for storage. When processing or data transfer is completed, the tape can be placed in off-line storage. Magnetic tape media come in several widths up to ½ inch and in many different lengths, some over 2000 feet. The QIC (QIC stands for quarter-inch cartridge) minicartridge can hold from 250 MB to 1 GB of data. However, the actual amount of data a given tape cartridge can store depends on the precision of the magnetic tape drive. Drives for ¼-inch tape cartridges, often called _ _ _ _ _ _ _ _ _ _ _ _ _ _ _ _ (_ _ _ _), store data in a _ _ _ _ _ _ _ _ _ _ _ manner using serial representation. A tape cartridge can be formatted to have from 4 to 60 tracks (depending on the precision of the tape drive). The read/write head reads or writes data to one, two, or four tracks at a time. A tape drive is rated by its storage capacity and its data transfer rate.

4-5

Safeguarding the content of your disks may be more important than safeguarding hardware. Someday you will be faced with hard disk failure or a damaged storage diskette. If you do not have your programs and data backed up properly, you may never be able to recreate what you had. This tragedy could easily cost you your grade in a class, your job or your business. The storage media for backup can be tape or disk. The three methods of backing up your files are full backup, selective backup, and modified files only backup. The frequency with which files are backed up depends on their volatility. When lost data is restored from a backup, the data that was changed during the time between the last backup and the data loss will have to be recreated. The size of hard disks installed in micros sold today makes full backup to diskette impractical. But, even if you do not have a TBU, you can still backup critical files to diskette.

4-6

Optical laser disk technology replaces the read/write head used by magnetic storage with two lasers. One writes data to the optical disk, and the other reads data from the disk. There are three types of optical laser disk systems used with today's computers: CD-ROM, WORM disks, and rewritable optical disks. Optical disk technology began with the recording industry and the CD which holds 74 minutes of music. The computer industry was quick to catch on. The CD-ROM is read-only-memory and, with its 680 MB storage capacity, is excellent for the integration of text, sound, graphics, motion video, and animation into multimedia applications. CD-ROMs store data in a single track that spirals from the center to the outside edge. Data are recorded on the CD-ROM's reflective surface in the form of pits and lands, and data pass over the movable laser detector at the same rate, no matter where the data are read. Popular CD-ROM drives are classified as double-spin, triple-spin, and quad-spin. However, even a quad-spin CD-ROM drive is slower than a magnetic hard disk drive. The introduction of multidisk player/changers, sometimes called _ _ _ _ _ _ _ _ _ , enables ready access to vast amounts of on-line data. CD-ROMs can be mass produced in the same manner that CDs are, and the storage cost per MB of data for CD- ROM is extremely cheap.

This rapid and universal acceptance of CD-ROM has given rise to an exciting new technology- _ _ -_ , _ _ _ _ _ _ _ _ _ _ _ _ -_ _ _ _ _ _ _ _ _ . A CD-R disk is functionally equivalent to a pre-recorded CD-ROM and will play in any CD-ROM drive. A _ _ -_ _ _ _ _ _ is used to write once to a CD-R disk to create an audio CD or a CD-ROM. For under $2000, commercial enterprises can expand the capabilities of a PC to create one-of-a-kind CDs or CD-ROMs at a fraction the cost of low-volume pressed disk manufacturing. Relatively inexpensive low-volume _ _ _ _ _ _ _ _ _ _ _ _ _ _ _ _ _ _ _ are used to duplicate locally produced CD-ROMs.

Write once, read many optical laser disks, or _ _ _ _ _ _ _ _ _ , are used by end user companies to store their own proprietary information. Like CD-ROMs, once the data have been written to the medium, they can only be read, not updated or changed. _ _ _ _ _ _ _ _ _ _ _ _ _ _ _ _ _ can store greater volumes of information than CD-ROM. Typically, WORM applications involve image processing or archival storage. The WORM disk cartridge, which has a data storage life in excess of 30 years, provides an alternative to magnetic tape for archival storage. The PC version of a WORM disk cartridge has a capacity of 600 MB.

_ use several technologies, including _ _ _ _ _ _ _ _ -_ _ _ _ _ _ _ _ _ _ _ _ _ _ _ , to integrate optical and magnetic disk technology to enable read-and-write storage. The 5¼-inch rewritable disk cartridges can store up to 1 GB. However, the technology must be improved before the optical disks can be considered as a direct alternative to magnetic media. Rewritable optical disks are beginning to find their niche. Applications that call for large volumes of storage with relatively little update activity are made to order for rewritable optical disks. Also, applications that require hardware to operate in harsh environments may be candidates for rewritable optical disks. As optical laser disk technology matures to offer reliable, cost-effective read/write operation, it eventually may dominate secondary storage in the future as magnetic disks and tape do today.

No one storage medium is ideal for all circumstances. Each has its strengths and weaknesses, and even these change with the different applications involved. RAM may be perfect storage and all that is needed for one application, but is certainly not for all applications due to its volatility. Price and size are just two of many considerations that must be made in selecting storage media.

4-7

Some scientists believe that holographic technology may give users everything they want in a storage device. Holographic memory systems enable the stacking of data on the recording surface. If nonvolatile chip technology continues to improve at the current pace, rotating storage may become obsolete. Already, flash memory chips are being developed that will have 16 times more storage capacity than the largest flash chips currently available. It's not unreasonable to expect 1 GB of flash memory in a PC by the end of the decade. We can expect at least one big leap in storage technology by the end of the century. That leap will forever change much of what we do and how we do it.

PRACTICE TEST

Multiple Choice *Circle the most appropriate answer.*

1. Computers use magnetic tape primarily for
   a.   random processing.
   b.   sequential processing, backup, and off-line storage.
   c.   Winchester disks.
   d.   sector processing, backup, and off-line storage.

2. In the mainframe environment, the most popular interchangeable storage media are
   a.   floppy disks.
   b.   diskettes.
   c.   hard or fixed disks.
   d.   headers.

3. A system for organizing data on a magnetic disk is
   a.   TPI organization.
   b.   sector and EOF organization.
   c.   dynamic flux rate (DFR) organization.
   d.   cylinder and sector organization.

4. A way to increase the number of programs that can be stored on a tape is to use
   a.   file compression.
   b.   data squeezing.
   c.   data representation.
   d.   data processing.

5. A 5¼-inch DS/DD floppy diskette has a maximum storage capacity of
   a.   360 KB.
   b.   360 kb.
   c.   360 mb.
   d.   360 MB.

6. A 3½-inch DS/DD diskette has a normal maximum storage capacity of
   a.   720 kb.
   b.   1.44 MB.
   c.   .72 MB.
   d.   1.2 mb.

7. The ¼-inch tape cartridge drives are often called
   a.   serpent tape drives.
   b.   tape backup units.
   c.   serial tape drives.
   d.   scenic tape drives.

8.   An optical laser disk technology which allows the user to write data to optical disk one time and subsequently read the data as often as is necessary is called a

a. CD-ROM.

b. WANG disk.

c. rewritable optical disk.

d. WORM disk.

9.   The magnetic tape cartridge is also called a

a. DASD cartridge.

b. serpentine cartridge.

c. serial cartridge.

d. data cartridge.

10.   Tape backup units (TBUs), store data in a

a. steamer manner.

b. random manner.

c. serpentine manner.

d. sector manner.

11.   A method of backup where only those files that have changed since the last backup are selected for back up to magnetic tape is referred to as

a. full backup.

b. modified files only backup.

c. sector backup.

d. selective backup.

12.   An undesired program that destroys data or damages hardware is commonly referred to as a

a. virus.

b. serpentine.

c. vaccine.

d. cylinder.

True – False *Circle T for true and F for false.*

13.   T F   Magnetic tape is sequential access only.

14.   T F   Another name for secondary storage is main memory.

15.   T F   Magnetic disks provide random access.

16.   T F   The number of characters per second that can be transmitted to primary storage is called the exchange rate.

17.   T F   Magneto-optical disk storage has both read and write capabilities.

18.   T F   Disk crashing is a technique that enhances system performance by placing programs and data that are likely to be called into RAM for processing from a disk into an area of RAM.

19.   T F   WORM optical laser disks would be an appropriate type of storage for an on-line hotel reservation system.

20.   T F   Optical laser disk technology is considered secondary storage.

21.   T F   Locating a particular song on an audio cassette tape is analogous to direct-access storage in a computer.

22.   T F   The two fundamental methods of storing and accessing data are random and sequential.

23.   T F   The storage medium for a tape drive is commonly called a tape pack.

24.   T F   Magnetic disks can be classified as interchangeable and fixed.

25.   T F   In reference to data storage media, the term tracks is a storage concept unique to magnetic tape and is not used in reference to magnetic disk storage media.

26.   T F   Storing data in sequential bit configurations is known as serial representation.

27.   T   F   The field allocation table on a magnetic disk tells the system where to find the files and directories stored on the disk.
28.   T   F   A source program file must be translated into machine language before a computer can execute the instructions it contains.
29.   T   F   Diskettes should be stored at temperatures between 50 and 125 degrees Celsius.
30.   T   F   Electronic bulletin-board systems are considered to be a common source of viral infection for computers.

Matching *Match the following terms with the appropriate definition or characteristic by placing the letter of the matching definition or characteristic in the blank.*

31.	_____ cylinder	(a)	A measurment based on the number of bits per unit area of disk surface
32.	_____ vaccine	(b)	A technique in which frequently referenced disk-based data are placed in an area of RAM that simulates disk storage
33.	_____ random access		
34.	_____ TPI	(c)	A type of computer program that is used to locate and eliminate computer viruses
35.	_____ WORM	(d)	The storage of bits one after another on a secondary storage medium
36.	_____ interchangeable magnetic disks	(e)	The number of tracks per inch of width of a magnetic disk surface
37.	_____ disk caching	(f)	Tape drive for 1/4-inch tape cartridges that stores data in a serpentine manner
38.	_____ serial representation	(g)	Disks stored off-line and loaded to the magnetic disk drives as they are needed
39.	_____ gigabyte	(h)	Direct access
40.	_____ TBU	(i)	A disk storage concept. Contrast with sector
41.	_____ disk density	(j)	A random-access secondary storage device
42.	_____ direct access storage device (DASD)	(k)	Write once, read many
		(l)	One billion bytes

Answers to Practice Test **1** b, **2** c, **3** a, **4** c, **5** d, **6** a, **7** b, **8** d, **9** d, **10** c, **11** b, **12** a, **13** t, **14** f, **15** t, **16** f, **17** t, **18** f, **19** f, **20** t, **21** f, **22** t, **23** f, **24** t, **25** f, **26** t, **27** f, **28** t, **29** f, **30** t, **31** i, **32** c, **33** h, **34** e, **35** k, **36** b, **37** g, **38** d, **39** l, **40** f, **41** a, **42** j.

CHAPTER CHECKUP

NAME		DATE	CHAPTER 4
COURSE	SECTION	INSTRUCTOR	

1. Explain why magnetic tape has become obsolete for online data processing and is now used primarily for backup and archival storage. *See section 4-4 of the text.*

2. Name two approaches to data manipulation and retrieval. *See section 4-2 of the text.*

■

■

3. Explain why tape backup units are said to store data in a serpentine manner. *See section 4-4 of the text.*

4. Explain the analogy drawn in the text between magnetic tape and audio cassette tape. *This should include a comparision of how data and content are stored and accessed on each. See section 4-2 of the text.*

5. Contrast "interchangeable" and "fixed disks." *See section 4-3 of the text.*

6. Briefly describe two sizes of interchangeable magnetic diskettes used with the PC. *See section 4-3 of the text.*

■

■

7. List the storage media term that matches each of the following phrases: *See section 4-3 of the text.*

(a)   a pie-shaped portion of a disk or diskette in which records are stored and subsequently retrieved

(b)   that portion of the disk that can be accessed without repositioning the read/write heads

(c)   that component of a disk drive or tape drive that reads from and writes to magnetic storage

(d)   the interval between when a computer makes a request for a transfer of data from secondary storage and when the operation is completed.

8. Explain the analogy drawn in the text between magnetic disk and compact disk. *See section 4-2 of the text.*

9. Briefly explain the concept of disk caching. *Disk caching speeds processing.*

10. All magnetic disk drives have an access arm. Why isn't one needed with optical laser disk storage? *The answer is in the name.*

11. Point out two differences between sequential and random processing. *See section 4-2 of the text.*

■

■

12. List the advantages and limitations of using CD-ROM. *See section 4-6 of the text.*

13. Explain why an interchangeable magnetic disk surface should not be touched or exposed to magnetic fields. *How is data represented on this data storage media?*

14. Briefly describe the purpose of file compression and how it works. *Remember the analogy to a sponge used in the text.*

15. What is a computer virus and what are the three most common sources of them. *A computer virus is not a living organism, although many of them act as though they were alive. See section 4-3 of the text.*

-
-
-
-

16. List and describe the three most popular methods used for backing up computer files. *One involves everything, another is where you choose, and the other one involves changes. See section 4-5 of the text.*

-
-
-

17. The formatting procedure causes the disk to be initialized with a recording format for your operating system. What specifically is done to the disk during this procedure? *This procedure is commonly referred to as formatting. Not only must a computer system be able to write to and read from a disk, it must also know where the files and data are on a disk. See section 4-3 of the text.*

18. List and briefly describe nine different types of computer files. *These are listed in section 4-1 of the text.*

■

■

■

■

■

■

■

■

19. List two types of optical data storage technology besides CD-ROM and explain how each is similar to and different from CD-ROM technology. *One type can only be written to once and another combines other technology with that of optical data storage to enable the user to write over existing data on the medium. See section 4-6 of the text.*

■

■

20.   Compose a multiple-choice, a true/false, and an essay question that you think would be appropriate for a quiz on this chapter.

M/C:

      (a)

      (b)

      (c)

      (d)

T/F:

Essay:

GRAPHICAL USER INTERFACE

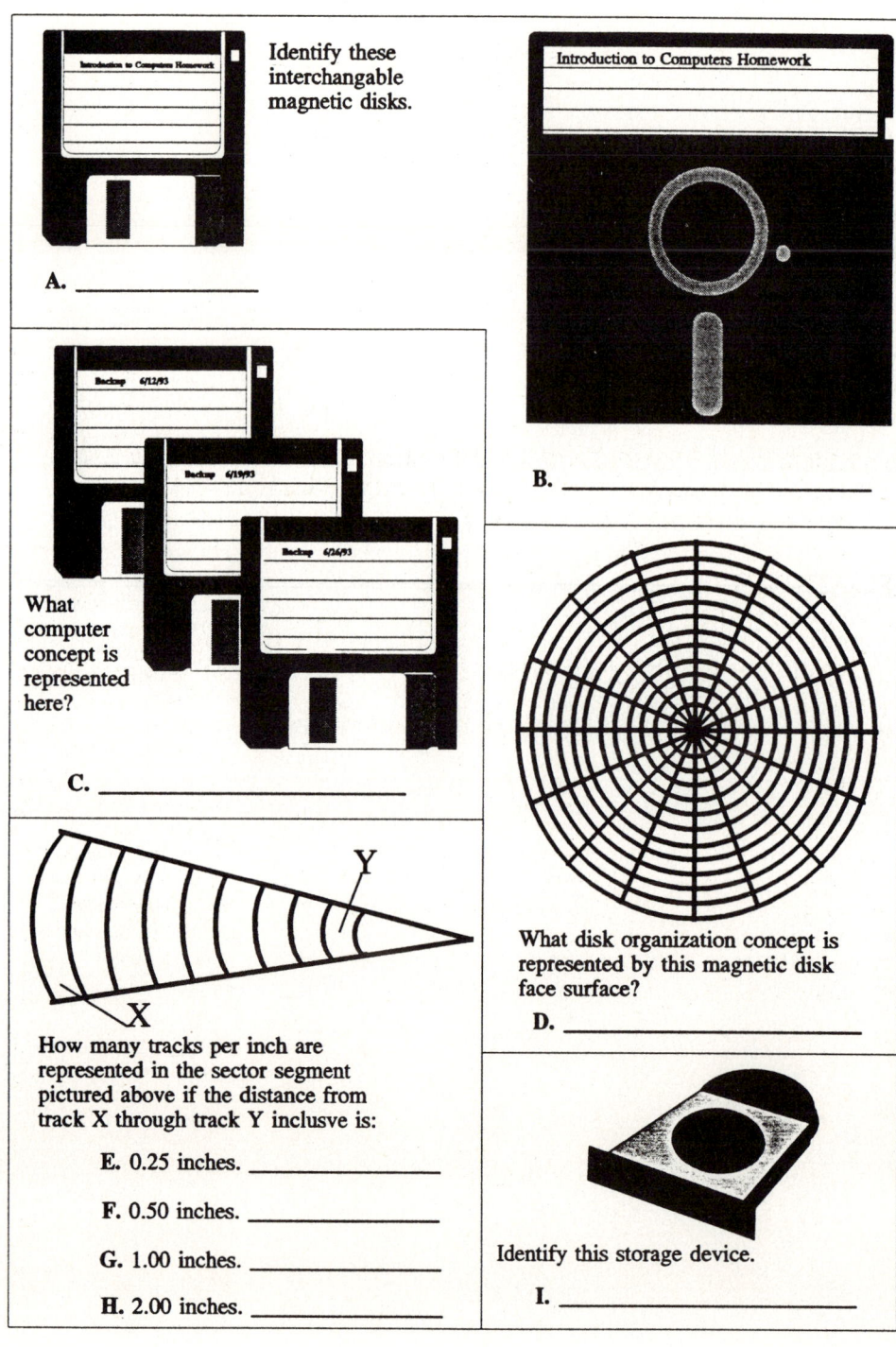

Identify these interchangable magnetic disks.

A. _____

B. _____

What computer concept is represented here?

C. _____

What disk organization concept is represented by this magnetic disk face surface?

D. _____

How many tracks per inch are represented in the sector segment pictured above if the distance from track X through track Y inclusve is:

E. 0.25 inches. _____

F. 0.50 inches. _____

G. 1.00 inches. _____

H. 2.00 inches. _____

Identify this storage device.

I. _____

**Chapter 5
Input/Output:
　　Computers in Action**

STUDENT LEARNING OBJECTIVES

- To explain alternative approaches to and devices for providing input to a system.
- To describe the operation and application of common output devices.
- To describe the use and characteristics of the different types of terminals.

VOCABULARY STUDY

acbadge reader
bar codes
cathode-ray tube
digital camera
digitize
digitizer tablet and pen
dot pitch
dot-matrix printer
flat-panel monitor
graphics adapter
graphics mode
gray scale
hydra printer
image processing
image scanner
ink-jet printer

joystick
landscape
laser printer
mouse pen
OCR (optical character recognition)
page printer
pixel
plotter
portrait
resolution
RGB monitor
scanner
screen image projector
smart card
source-data automation

speech synthesis
speech-recognition system
telephony
text mode
touch-screen monitor
trackball
trackpad
trackpoint
turnaround document
video RAM (VRAM)
vision-input system
voice-response system
wand scanner
X terminal

INTERACTIVE REVIEW

Use the terms in the Vocabulary Study to fill in the following blanks. You will only use each term once. You may need to insert a plural form of a term or adjust its verb tense. Check your answers with the chapter material and the glossary in your textbook.

5-1

Input devices translate data into a form the computer understands. Output devices translate the binary language of computers into a form we can understand. We interface with computers in many ways besides with a keyboard, mouse, and monitor.

5-2

The primary input device for computers today and for the foreseeable future is the keyboard. The standard for the PC is the 101 keyboard with the QWERTY layout. However, there are many special-function keyboards in many applications like fast food restaurants. In addition to keyboards, point-and-draw devices are widely used. The mouse is the most popular with the PC, but there are also many others in general use. One that uses a stick to move the graphics cursor is the _ _ _ _ _ _ _ _ . The _ _ _ _ _ _ _ _ is essentially an upside down mouse. The _ _ _ _ _ _ _ _ is rolled across the desktop like a mouse and held like a pen. The _ _ _ _ _ _ _ _ _ _ _ _ _ _ _ _ _ _ uses a stylus or crosshair device with a pressure sensitive tablet. To maintain maximum portability, laptops often have point-and-draw devices built in. Positioned in or near the laptop's keyboard, _ _ _ _ _ _ _ _ _ _ _ function like miniature joysticks but are operated with the tip of the finger. Simply move your finger about a touch-sensitive pad on a _ _ _ _ _ _ _ _ to move the graphics cursor. There are many more point and draw devices too numerous to mention and many more variations on the ones mentioned. Can you name some of them?

5-3

_ _ _ _ _ _ _ - _ _ _ _ _ _ _ _ _ _ _ _ helps to minimize key entry transcription of data. Using a laser scanner to read _ _ _ _ _ _ _ on packages is one example. A variety of _ _ _ _ _ _ _ _ read and interpret information on printed matter and convert it to a format that can be interpreted by a computer. _ (_ _ _) is also being used and constantly improved. This is where data in machine-readable format are entered directly from the original source document. OCR and bar code scanners use either contact or laser technology. These devices can "learn" to read almost any typeface or bar code. They are divided into three basic categories, hand-held label or _ _ _ _ _ _ _ _ _ _ _ _ , stationary label scanners, and document scanners. Stationary scanners and bar codes used with the Universal Product Code (UPC) and in supermarkets are probably the most well recognized source-data automation systems. There are many other applications for optical scanners besides in grocery stores. The generation and use of a _ _ _ _ _ _ _ _ _ _ _ _ _ _ _ _ _ like those used for utility bills, high-speed data gathering, such as automated toll booths, and credit card purchases using original-source data collection are just a few. How many more can you think of? An _ _ _ _ _ _ _ _ _ _ _ is used to translate, or _ _ _ _ _ _ _ _ _ , an image into an electronic format. This type of scanner is available in hand or page models and can be either gray scale or color. _ _ _ _ _ _ _ _ _ _ _ _ _ is the retrieval and manipulation of images stored on a computer. Image scanners are classified as either page scanners or hand scanners. Image scanners also scan and interpret the alphanumeric characters on regular printed pages using sophisticated OCR software. Image processing is beccomming a popular method for eliminating paper in businesses and even the home. Documents can be digitized and then stored electronically in a fraction of the space necessary for the original paper documents.

Magnetic stripes have been used for years now to store data on the backs of credit cards and for entry to ATMs. The data stored on these stripes are read into a computer with a _ _ _ _ _ _ _ _ _ _ _ . An enhanced version of the magnetic stripe card is the _ _ _ _ _ _ _ _ _ which contains a microprocessor for data storage.

_ _ _ _ _ _ - _ _ _ _ _ _ _ _ _ _ _ _ _ _ _ _ are able to recognize spoken words. Most of these systems are speaker-dependent. The system uses a four-step process: say the word, digitize the word, match the word using templates, and display the word or perform the command. The templates used form the database of the system. The creation of these databases is called training. When combined with an audio response unit or speech synthesizer, the conversation can become two-way. A _ _ _ _ _ _ - _ _ _ _ _ _ _ _ _ uses a digitizing camera and a computer to recognize and identify objects. At present, these systems are best suited to very specialized tasks involving only a few images, such as quality control inspection on an assembly line. As prices of _ _ _ _ _ _ _ _ _ _ _ _ _ _ drop, they may soon replace traditional photographic film with diskettes or CD-R. Certain limited applications are also well suited for hand-held data entry devices. A typical device would have a limited keyboard, a calculator-like display, data storage capability, and a scanning device. Data collected on such a device, like taking inventory of a warehouse or retail store, are uploaded to a host computer for further processing.

5-4

Basically, output devices translate the language of computers into the language of humans. Output comes in two forms. Monitors, screen image projectors, and voice response units produce soft copy output. Printers, plotters, and desktop film recorders produce hard copy output. Monitors are defined by graphics adapter, size, resolution, color, and display quality. The _ _ _ _ _ _ _ _ _ _ _ _ _ _ _ is the device controller for the monitor. Most graphics adapters are inserted into an expansion slot on the motherboard. Some, however, are built into the motherboard. Graphics adapters have their own RAM, called _ _ _ _ _ _ _ _ , or (_ _ _ _), where they prepare monitor-bound images for display. Monitor sizes range from 5 to 30 inches, diagonal screen measurement. The quality of a monitor's output is a function of its _ _ _ _ _ _ _ _ _ _ , the number of addressable points on the screen. These addressable points are called _ _ _ _ _ _ _ , short for picture elements. PC displays are in one of two modes. A simple word processing package would operate in _ _ _ _ _ _ _ _ , whereas a GUI would operate in _ _ _ _ _ _ _ _ _ _ _ . A monitor's resolution may also be described in terms of its _ _ _ _ _ _ _ _ _ , or the distance between the centers of adjacent pixels. The crispness of the image improves as the dot pitch gets smaller. Monochrome monitors display images in only one color, but they can display in shades of that color called _ _ _ _ _ _ _ _ _ _ . Most color monitors mix red, green, and blue to achieve a spectrum of colors, and are called _ _ _ _ _ _ _ _ _ _ _ . The four most popular monitors are CGA, EGA, VGA, and SVGA. Two more considerations that affect the quality of a monitor's display are the refresh rate and if the monitor is interlaced or non-interlaced. LCD (liquid crystal display), gas plasma, and EL (electroluminescent) technologies are used in space-saving, _ _ _ _ - _ _ _ _ _ _ _ _ _ _ _ _ _ . Each of these technologies has its advantages and disadvantages. By allowing the user to choose from available options by simply touching the desired icon or menu item with their finger, _ _ _ _ _ - _ _ _ _ _ _ _ _ _ _ _ _ permit input as well as output.

When purchasing a printer, the major considerations are price, color or black and white, volume of output, quality of output, special features needed, and network considerations. Three basic technologies dominate the PC printer arena: dot-matrix, ink jet, and page. Printers and software packages allow the user to orient their output in _ _ _ _ _ _ _ _ or _ _ _ _ _ _ _ _ _ images. Printers can be categorized as either impact or nonimpact. A popular impact printer used with the PC is the _ _ _ - _ _ _ _ _ _ _ _ _ _ _ which forms characters one at a time using pins striking a ribbon as the print head moves, usually bidirectionally, across the paper. Its speed is measured in characters per second (cps) and most generally has a tractor feed for continuous-form paper and an automatic sheet feeder option available for large volumes of single-sheet paper. The print quality of these printers is rated from draft to near-letter-quality (NLQ), and some even have color ribbons available for limited color output. Dot-matrix line printers are similar to matrix printers with moving print heads except that they have a row of pins running the width of the page and print a full line of dots at a time, and produce a much larger volume of output in a considerably shorter period of time. Their speed is measured in lines per minute (lpm). Impact printers, as opposed to nonimpact printers, touch the paper and can produce carbon copies along with the original. _ _ _ _ _ _ _ _ _ _ _ _ _ are nonimpact and use a variety of technologies to achieve high-speed output by printing a page at a time. Page printers are also referenced simply as _ _ _ _ _ _ _ _ _ _ _ _ _ . Their speed is rated in pages per minute (ppm). The most popular employ laser, LED (light-emitting diode), LCS (liquid crystal shutter), and other laser -like technology. Most page printers are monochrome, but color page printer technology is rapidly becoming more affordable. Desktop page printers are capable of speeds of up to 32 ppm and are capable of letter-quality (LQ) and near-typeset-quality (NTQ) output. The resolution of low-end desktop page printers is 300 dots per inch (dpi). 600 to 1200 dpi desktops are becoming more affordable. Desktop page printers have added significant fuel to the recent explosion of desktop publishing.

Although the output quality of _ _ _ - _ _ _ _ _ _ _ _ _ is more in line with page printers, their mechanical operation is more like that of the dot-matrix printer. Just as the dot-matrix pins hit the ribbon and paper, several independently controlled injection chambers squirt ink droplets on the paper. Resolutions for the typical ink-jet printer approach that of a 300-dpi page printer. Some newer models boast resolutions in excess of 700 dpi. A significant advantage of ink-jet printers is a low purchase price for the ability to produce good quality color output. The ink-jet printer is lower in price than a page printer, but the cost per page of output is usually higher. Mainframe-based page printers operate with the same basic technology as do desktop page printers except they produce output much faster. A new development in printers that combines several functions such as photocopying, page printing, and page scanning, is called the _ _ _ _ _ _ _ _ _ _ _ . Look for these to be the most popular office addition within the next few years.

There are two basic types of _ _ _ _ _ _ _ _ -the drum plotter and the flatbed plotter. In using both, the computer is used to control several pens which vary the width and color of the line and produce high precision, graphic hard copy. Presentation graphics can be created on a computer and then projected onto a large screen with a _ _ _ _ _ _ _ _ _ _ _ _ _ _ _ _ _ _ _ . There are two types of _ _ _ _ _ _ _ _ _ _ _ _ _ _ _ _ _ _ _ . One uses a reproduction of a human voice and other sounds, and the other uses _ _ _ _ _ _ _ _ _ _ _ _ _ _ _ _ . The first type of unit uses digitized recordings of actual sounds stored in a database. The other produces speech by mixing sounds resembling the phonemes that make up speech. Eventually, as speech recognition and voice response systems are improved, we will be able to use computers as translators for conversations between foreign languages.

5-5

The two most popular general-purpose terminals for remote computer systems are the video display terminal (VDT) and the telephone. The VDT uses a keyboard similar to that of a PC for input and a _ _ _ _ _ _ _ _ _ _ _ _ _ or monitor for soft copy output. Most terminals have little or no processing capabilities and are often referred to as dumb terminals. Terminals that have processing capabilities and RAM, oftentimes comparable to PCs and workstations, are called _ - _ _ _ _ _ _ _ _ _ . These terminals can run multiple applications and allow users to interact with the computer system through GUIs and are always configured with some type of point and draw device. The telephone is becoming increasingly popular as a computer terminal. A combination of the telephone's touch-tone keypad, voice input, and voice output can be used for effective complex interaction with a computer system. When linked to a computer, potential applications for the telephone abound. _ _ _ _ _ _ _ _ _ is the integration of computers and telephones, the two most essential instruments of business. Telephony promotes efficient interactions and as it matures, many routine communications will be handled entirely by computers. There is also a considerable number of special function terminals such as automatic teller machines and point-of-sale (POS) terminals.

PRACTICE TEST

Multiple Choice *Circle the letter of the most appropriate answer.*

1. Vision-input systems are best suited for tasks in which
    a.   many images are encountered.
    b.   few images are encountered.
    c.   voice-data entry is required.
    d.   the reject bin is large.
2. Primary attributes of monitors include
    a.   resolution, size, and processing speed.
    b.   size, color, and serial ports.
    c.   color, size, and resolution.
    d.   color, processing speed, and resolution.
3. Which of the following groups are considered as input-only devices?
    a.   mouse, track ball, and joy stick
    b.   pen plotter, mouse, and light pen
    c.   plotter, terminal, and mouse
    d.   bar code, OCR, printer
4. Which of the following printers uses tiny pins to form characters?
    a.   laser
    b.   dot matrix
    c.   daisy wheel
    d.   page
5. Which of the following technologies is common with laptop monitors?
    a.   RBG
    b.   CAD
    c.   LCD
    d.   GPQ
6. A speaker-independent, voice-data-entry computer system
    a.   is not technologically possible.
    b.   uses no database.
    c.   has an unlimited vocabulary.
    d.   can have many users.
7. A device that produces computer voice output is called a
    a.   voice-reproduction unit.
    b.   voice-response unit.
    c.   voice-recognition unit.
    d.   voice-activation unit.
8. Which of the following eliminates the need for keystrokes to enter data into a computer?
    a.   bar files
    b.   CRT units
    c.   bar codes
    d.   ink jets
9. Another name for a terminal is
    a.   VTD.
    b.   video display terminal.
    c.   the video toaster.
    d.   cathode liquid display.
10. Which of the following devices is considered to be an output only device?
    a.   hydra printer   c.   PDA
    b.   monitor   d.   plotter

11.   Page printers are often referred to as
        a.   impact printers.
        b.   offset printers.
        c.   nonimpact printers.
        d.   liquid image transfer printers.
12.   The type of credit card that contains a microprocessor is called a
        a.   digitizer.
        b.   smart card.
        c.   badge reader.
        d.   hydra card.

True - False *Circle T next to each true statement and F next to each false statement.*

13.   T F   A terminal's primary input device is the keyboard and its primary soft-copy output
                device is usually the printer.
14.   T F   The trend in data entry is toward decreasing the number of transcription steps needed
                to get data into machine-readable form.
15.   T F   The mouse is an output device found on some microcomputers.
16.   T F   PC displays are in either text mode or graphics mode.
17.   T F   OCR is an acronym for oral computer response, a voice response system.
18.   T F   A desktop page printer prints faster than a impact matrix printer.
19.   T F   Recent development of the hydra printer has been largely responsible for major
                advancements in source-data automation in the retail trade industry.
20.   T F   Hand-held data entry devices are usually off-line.
21.   T F   An "intelligent" card, the update to the magnetic stripe-based card, is called the gold
                card.
22.   T F   A voice-response unit translates human speech into a form of input that a computer
                can understand.
23.   T F   The joystick, track ball, digitizer tablet and pen, and mouse are point-and-draw
                devices.
24.   T F   The hydra printer gets its name from the water-based ink transfer technology that it
                uses for producing printed materials.
25.   T F   An ATM is both an input device and an output device.
26.   T F   A plotter is a computer input device that uses a stylus and a pressure sensitive pad to
                transfer data to the computer.
27.   T F   RGB codes are the basis for the UPC system.
28.   T F   The traditional key layout for the letter keys on a 101-keyboard is commonly referred
                to as QUERTY.
29.   T F   Trackpoints function like miniature joysticks operated with the tip of the finger.
30.   T F   At supermarket checkout counters using bar codes, the checker passes the bar code on
                a product over a laser printer.

Matching *Match the following terms with the appropriate definition or characteristic by placing the letter of the matching definition or characteristic in the blank.*

31. ____ resolution

32. ____ RGB

33. ____ desktop page printers

34. ____ ppm

35. ____ source data automation

36. ____ badge reader

37. ____ CRT

38. ____ pixel

39. ____ text mode

40. ____ portrait

41. ____ vision-input system

42. ____ wand scanner

(a) entering data at the source

(b) An addressable point on a display screen to which light can be directed under program control

(c) Refers to the orientation of the print on a page

(d) A mode of operation for PC monitors

(e) The video monitor component of a terminal

(f) Magnetic stripes

(g) A device that enables limited visual input to a computer system.

(h) Hand-held OCR input device.

(i) Referring to the number of addressable points on a terminal's screen

(j) Laser printers fall into this category

(k) color monitor

(l) pages per minute

Answers to Practice Test **1** b, **2** c, **3** a, **4** b, **5** c, **6** d, **7** b, **8** c, **9** b, **10** d, **11** c, **12** b, **13** f, **14** t, **15** f, **16** t, **17** f, **18** t, **19** f, **20** t, **21** f, **22** f, **23** t, **24** f, **25** t, **26** f, **27** f, **28** f, **29** t, **30** f, **31** i, **32** k, **33** j, **34** l, **35** a, **36** f, **37** e, **38** b, **39** d, **40** c, **41** g, **42** h.

CHAPTER CHECKUP

NAME		DATE	CHAPTER 5
COURSE	SECTION	INSTRUCTOR	

1. What is the purpose of input and output devices? *See section 5-1 of the text.*

2. List and briefly describe two point-and-draw devices. *See section 5-2 of the text.*

■

■

3. What is the trend in data entry? Give an example. *See section 5-3 of the text.*

4. List and briefly describe three types of OCR scanners. *See section 5-3 of the text.*

■

■

■

5. Describe one application of optical scanners. *See section 5-3 of the text.*

6. Name the two types of image scanners. Which has the highest resolution? *See section 5-3 of the text.*

■

■

7. Describe briefly how a smart card works. *See section 5-3 of the text.*

8. A speech-recognition system is an example of an input or output device? A speech synthesizer is an example of an input or output device? *See section 5-3 and section 5-4 of the text.*

9. What type of tasks are best suited for vision-input systems? *See section 5-3 of the text.*

10. List four common "output-only" devices. (All types of printers count as only one output device.) *See section 5-4 of the text.*

-

-

-

-

11. What are three primary attributes of monitors? *See section 5-4 of the text.*

-

-

-

12. Classify each of the following types of printers as either impact (I) or nonimpact (N) printer. *See section 5-4 of the text.*

(a) page printer

(b) line dot-matrix printer

(c) serial dot-matrix printer

(d) ink-jet printer

13. What application would an impact dot-matrix printer be better suited for than would a laser printer? Why? *See section 5-4 of the text.*

14. Why are ink-jet printers usually quieter in operation than impact dot-matrix printers? *See section 5-4 of the text.*

15. How might a marketing manager make use of the capabilities of plotters? *Marketing managers are interested in sales patterns.*

16. One of the more interesting future applications of voice response and speech recognition devices will be in the cockpit of sophisticated jet fighters. Research in this area will ultimately be translated to applications on the factory floor. Describe a factory situation where speech recognition devices might be applicable. *See section 5-3 and section 5-4 of the text.*

17. An automatic teller machine (ATM) is an example of a special-function terminal. Where else have you seen special-function terminals? *See section 5-5 of the text.*

18. Describe the differences between a dumb terminal and an X-terminal. *One has its own processing capabilities and the other must rely on the host computer for processing capabilities. See section 5-5 of the text.*

19. What differentiates a hydra printer from a traditional desktop page printer? *The term hydra comes from Greek mythology. The Hydra was a creature with many heads. Could the concept of many heads be related to the concept of many functions? See section 5-4 of the text.*

20. Compose a multiple-choice, a true/false, and an essay question that you think would be appropriate for a quiz on this chapter.

M/C:
(a)
(b)
(c)
(d)
T/F:
Essay:

GRAPHICAL USER INTERFACE

Identify each of the following within the context of computer based input/output. (Hint: The first two refer to print formats. Letter D answer is short for picture element. Letter F is a point-and-draw device.)

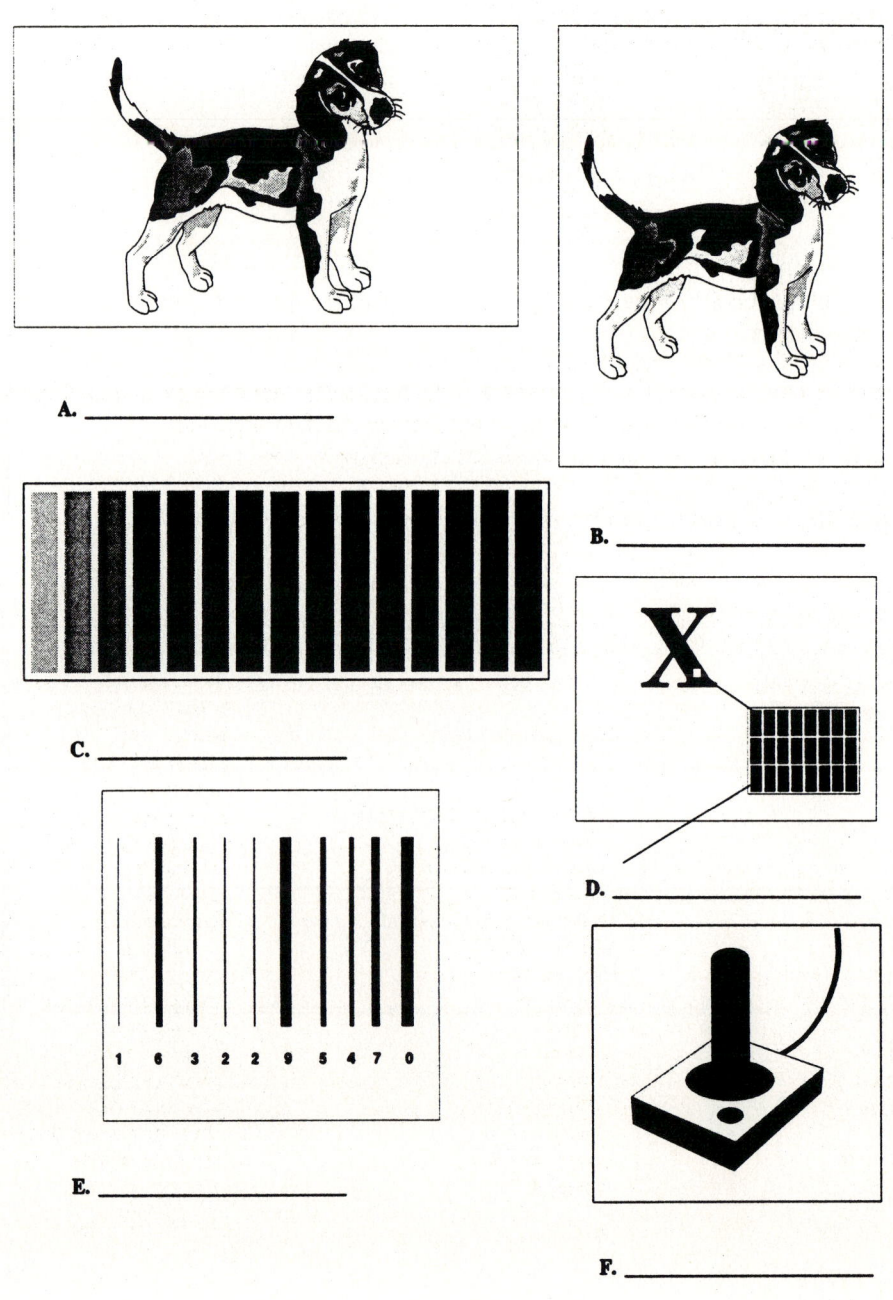

A. _____

B. _____

C. _____

D. _____

E. _____

F. _____

Chapter 6
Networks and
Networking: Linking
the World

STUDENT LEARNING OBJECTIVES

- To describe the concept of connectivity.
- To demonstrate an understanding of data communications terminology and applications.
- To detail the function and operation of data communications hardware.
- To describe alternatives and sources of data transmission services.
- To illustrate the various kinds of network topologies.
- To describe a local area network and its associated hardware and software.

VOCABULARY STUDY

basynchronous transmission
back-end applications software
backbone
baud
bits per second (bps)
bus topology
client computer
client/server computing
coaxial cable
common carrier
communications channel
communications protocol
communications server
connectivity
CSMA/CD access method
cooperative processing
data communications
dial-up line
digital convergence
downsizing

electronic data interchange (EDI)
electronic messaging
fiber optic cable
file server
front-end applications software
front-end processor
geosynchronous orbit
handshaking
Integrated Services Digital Network (ISDN)
LAN operating system
LAN server
leased line
local net
message
microwave signals
multiplexer
network address
network bus

network interface card (NIC)
network topology
node
peer-to-peer LAN
print server
private line
radio signals
ring topology
router
server computer
star topology
switched line
synchronous transmission
telecommunications
tiny area network (TAN)
token access method
twisted-pair wire
wide area network (WAN)
wireless transceiver

INTERACTIVE REVIEW

Use the terms in the Vocabulary Study to fill in the following blanks. You will only use each term once. You may need to insert a plural form of a term or adjust its verb tense. Check your answers with the chapter material and the glossary in your textbook.

6-1

Knowledge workers today rely on computer networks to retrieve and share information in a timely manner. To do so requires that computer systems achieve some degree of _____ . The ideal situation for complete access to and sharing of information would be to achieve total connectivity. However, this ideal is still several years away. _____ _____ , or _____ the collection and distribution of the electronic representation of information from and to remote facilities, is required to achieve connectivity. We are going through a period of _____ _____ . TVs, PCs, telephones, movies, infomercials, college textbooks, newspapers, and much, much more are converging toward digital compatibility. The raw data are digitized and transmitted over a variety of transmission media. Intracompany networking is one form of what is often referred to as _____ _____ . Intercompany networking, or _____ ____ _____ (___), is another.

6-2

A modem, or modulator-demodulator, is needed to transmit data over telephone lines. The internal type is an add-on card. The external type is connected to the computer via a port. There are also fax modems which enable a computer to communicate with a remote fax machine.

Computers that are required to process several tasks at the same time are designed to distribute their processing load among several special-function processors. The host processor is responsible for overall system control. A _____ is sent by the source and received by the destination. The link established by the _____-___ _____ between the two is referred to as _____ . Each element in a computer network that can serve as a source or destination is assigned a _____ _____ . These addresses are required for the front-end processor to properly route messages through the network. Data from low speed devices are often concentrated by a _____ , which is used to handle data communications processing details between the CPU and remote devices.

The problem prohibiting total connectivity is compatibility of communications and processing operations between different computer systems and software. _____ _____ are rules established to govern the way data are transmitted in a computer network. Because networks use a variety of communications protocols and operating systems, incompatible networks cannot "talk" directly to one another. The compatibility gap between various types of networks is bridged by a _____ . A system of routers and the associated transmission media that links the routers and the mainframe computers within a multi-network system is called a _____ .

6-3

A _____ _____ is the facility through which electronic signals are transmitted between locations in a computer network. A channel's capacity is rated in ____ ___ _____ (___). The term ____ is also often used when discussing a channel's capacity, but means the same thing when used in this context. Telephone lines are often used for data communications. Most telephone lines are rated at 28,800 bps, but 1540 K bps data rates are available through _____ _____ such as American Telephone & Telegraph. The old _____-____ ____ is the transmission media used to link your home or office telephone with the telephone system. A transmission media of electrical wire permitting high speed transmission with minimal signal distortion is called _____ _____ . Hairlike _____ _____ _____ carries data as laser-generated light beams faster than their copper-wire counterparts. Communications channels do not have to be wires or fibers. Data can also be transmitted via _____ _____ or other _____ _____ . Microwave radio signals are used

to transmit data to communications satellites in _ _ _ _ _ _ _ _ _ _ _ _ _ _ _ _ _ _ , and ground
based receivers and repeaters with line-of-sight transmissions. Wireless transceivers eliminate the need
for a physical link between addresses in a computer network. Common carriers provide long distance
data communications to individuals and companies through either a _ _ _ _ _ _ _ _ _ _ (or
_ _ _ _ _ _ _ _ _ _) or a _ _ _ _ _ _ _ _ _ _ _ _ (or _ _ _ - _ _ _ _ _). Some common
carriers offer a source-to-destination digital alternative using the _ _ _ _ _ _ _ _ _ _ _ _ _ _ _ _ _ _
_ _ _ _ _ _ _ _ _ _ _ _ _ _ (_ _ _ _) telecommunications standard. There is no need for modems in
ISDN communication.

6-4

A _ _ _ _ is an end point in a computer network. These end points are connected using one
or more of the three basic _ _ _ _ _ _ _ _ _ _ _ _ _ _ _ _ _ _ . Smaller computer systems communicate
with each other through the host computer and usually share the host computer's database when
connected by the _ _ _ _ _ _ _ _ _ _ _ _ . No one computer is the central focal point in the _ _ _ _
_ _ _ _ _ _ _ _ . A central cable called a _ _ _ _ _ _ _ _ _ _ is used in the _ _ _ _ _ _ _ _ _ _ .
Most computer networks are hybrids composed of combinations of the basic topologies.

PCs and workstations offer more computing capacity per dollar than mainframe computers. This
has resulted in the development of _ _ _ _ _ _ _ / _ _ _ _ _ _ _ _ _ _ _ _ _ _ which is a form of
distributed processing where data are downloaded to the _ _ _ _ _ _ _ _ _ _ _ _ _ from the
_ _ _ _ _ _ _ _ _ _ _ _ _ and uploaded to the server from the client when the client has completed
processing. The client computer runs _ _ _ _ _ _ - _ that
performs processing associated with the user interface and applications processing that can be done
locally. The server computer's _ _ _ _ _ - _ performs
processing tasks in support of its clients. This trend toward smaller central computers and distributed
processing is called _ _ _ _ _ _ _ _ _ _ _ .

Communications protocols are defined in layers. The first, or physical layer defines the manner
in which network nodes are connected. Data that are transmitted at irregular intervals in
_ are required to have start/stop bits at the beginning and
end of data to be transmitted. In _ , start/stop bits are not
required because all transmissions occur at timed intervals.

6-5

A _ _ _ _ _ _ _ _ _ _ _ _ _ _ _ _ _ (_ _ _) connects nodes in widely dispersed geographic
areas, and a local area network (LAN), or _ _ _ _ _ _ _ _ _ connects nodes in close proximity. The
local net, including all data communications channels, is owned by the organization using it. The
_ _ _ _ _ _ _ _ _ _ _ _ _ _ or _ _ _ describes a very small network with as few as two nodes. In
practice, PCs and workstations provide the foundation for local area networks. LANs make good
business sense because available resources such as applications software, mainframe links,
communications capabilities, I/O devices, storage devices, and add-on boards can be shared. The access
method controlling node communications is embedded in the ROM on the _ _ _ _ _ _ _
_ _ _ _ _ _ _ _ _ _ _ _ _ (_ _ _). Only one node on a LAN can send information at any given time.
When a LAN with a ring topology uses the _ _ _ _ _ _ _ _ _ _ _ _ _ _ _ _ , an electronic token
travels around a ring of nodes in the form of a header. Think of the token as a benevolent dictator who,
when captured, bestows the privilege of sending a transmission. In the _ _ _ _ / _ _ _ _ _ _ _ _
_ _ _ _ _ _ _ , nodes on the LAN must contend for the right to send a message. If the line is busy, the
sending computer keeps trying to send until the line is free.

Twisted pair, coaxial, and fiber optic cables are commonly used in the physical connections
between network nodes. In wireless transmission, the cable runs from the transceiver to the NIC. LAN
servers include the _ _ _ _ _ _ _ _ _ _ _ , _ _ _ _ _ _ _ _ _ _ , and _ _ _ _ _ _ _ _ _ _ _ _ _ _ _
_ _ _ _ _ _ _ . A dedicated server can be a standard micro or a micro constructed to operate specifically
as a _ _ _ _ _ _ _ _ . _ _ _ _ _ _ _ _ _ _ _ _ _ _ _ _ _ _ are the nucleus of a local net. In a
_ _ _ _ _ - _ _ - _ _ _ _ _ _ _ , all PCs are equal with any PC serving as a client or server at any given
time. Two popular peer-to-peer LAN operating systems are Microsoft's Windows for Workgroups and
Artisoft's LANtastic. In a dedicated server LAN, specific micros act as servers all the time. Two popular

LAN operating systems are Novell's NetWare and Microsoft's LAN Manager. LANs enable the sharing of general-purpose software, such as WordPerfect (word processing) and Excel (spreadsheet). There is also a sizeable amount of software written specifically for use on a LAN called groupware in the marketplace today, and more is on the way. E-mail is probably the best known of these. Networks are poping up everywhere. Where once the portable computer was considered to be an amazing technological advancement, we now have portable networks.

PRACTICE TEST

Multiple Choice *Circle the letter of the most appropriate answer.*

1. Which of these is not a transmission medium for data communications?
   a. microwave
   b. convection
   c. telephone lines
   d. fiber optic cable

2. Electronic data interchange
   a. worsens relations between trading partners.
   b. increases errors and correction costs.
   c. reduces paper-processing costs and delays.
   d. exaggerates receivables and inventory disputes.

3. Companies that strive toward connectivity do all of the following except
   a. enable a page printer to service a network of microcomputers.
   b. share information resources.
   c. enable incompatible computers to communicate.
   d. drop plans for EFT applications.

4. The front-end processor in a computer network is responsible for
   a. overall computer system control.
   b. establishing a handshake between network nodes.
   c. concentrating data from low speed devices.
   d. the execution of computer applications or programs.

5. When communicating via a front-end processor, each computer system in a network is assigned
   a. a ROM number.
   b. an internet address.
   c. a network address.
   d. a traffic-control system.

6. One format for a LAN operating system is
   a. peer-to-peer.
   b. common server.
   c. place-to-place.
   d. CSMA/CD.

7. A popular access method for computer networks is
   a. Ethylnet.
   b. bus token.
   c. token ring.
   d. pier-to-pier.

8. Which of the following is not a hardware component of a LAN?
   a. file server
   b. NIC
   c. monitor server
   d. coaxial cable

9. Which of the following is not a basic computer network topology?
   a. train topology
   b. bus topology
   c. star topology
   d. ring topology
10. The multiplexer is not a
    a. device that transmits data from a number of sources over a single communications channel.
    b. device that concentrates data.
    c. multiplexer.
    d. smart card.
11. Which communications protocol is used for high-speed data transmission between computers?
    a. asynchronous
    b. synchronous
    c. microwave
    d. geosynchronous
12. The interfacing of diverse sets of hardware, software, and databases is commonly referred to as
    a. digital conveyance.
    b. handshaking.
    c. connectivity.
    d. digitizing.

True - False *Circle T next to each true statement and F next to each false statement.*

13. T F   A device called a module modulates and demodulates signals for data communications.
14. T F   A multiplexer is a processor in a computer network that is located down-line from the host and front-end processor.
15. T F   Connectivity refers to the degree to which hardware devices can be functionally linked to one another.
16. T F   The term peer-to-peer describes a network access method.
17. T F   AT&T and Western Union are examples of common carriers.
18. T F   Communications satellites have made our society less dependent on data communications.
19. T F   Modems are needed for data communications via telephone lines because telephone lines were designed for voice transmission, not data transmission.
20. T F   The front-end processor establishes the link between the destination and the end-user.
21. T F   Electronic data interchange uses computers and data communications to transmit data electronically between companies.
22. T F   Computer network topologies include star, token, bus, and hybrid topologies.
23. T F   An electronic mail application allows you to send electronic mail to other users on the network.
24. T F   A microcomputer can serve as a terminal linked to a mainframe.
25. T F   Constructivity is the term used to describe the degree of data communications that exists between two computer systems.
26. T F   Communications protocols are rules governing the way to run an information system.
27. T F   The acronym LAN stands for log-on area network.
28. T F   The term token-ring refers to a popular LAN access method.
29. T F   Fiber optic cable can carry both voice and digital signals.
30. T F   The network access method is embedded in the ROM on the network interlink card.

Matching *Match the following terms with the appropriate definition or characteristic by placing the letter of the matching definition or characteristic in the blank.*

31.	_____ handshaking	(a)	Local area network
32.	_____ baud	(b)	Electrical wire constructed to permit high-speed data transmission
33.	_____ network topologies	(c)	Data that are loaded from a mainframe to micros for processing
34.	_____ coaxial cable	(d)	A central cable used in the bus topology
35.	_____ download	(e)	Star, ring, and bus
36.	_____ asynchronous transmission	(f)	Transmission of these signals is line-of-sight
37.	_____ common carriers	(g)	Enables a PC to perform fax machine functions
38.	_____ fax modem	(h)	A computer network communications protocol that transmits data at irregular intervals
39.	_____ local net	(i)	Would include e-mail application
40.	_____ transmission medium	(j)	Sprint, MCI, AT&T
41.	_____ microwave radio signal	(k)	Process used to establish the link between source and destination
42.	_____ groupware	(l)	Often used interchangeably with bits per second

Answers to Practice Test **1** b, **2** c, **3** d, **4** b, **5** c, **6** d, **7** c, **8** c, **9** a, **10** d, **11** b, **12** c, **13** f, **14** t, **15** t, **16** f, **17** t, **18** f, **19** t, **20** t, **21** t, **22** f, **23** t, **24** t, **25** f, **26** t, **27** f, **28** t, **29** t, **30** f, **31** k, **32** l, **33** e, **34** b, **35** c, **36** h, **37** j, **38** g, **39** a, **40** d, **41** f, **42** i.

CHAPTER CHECKUP

NAME		DATE	CHAPTER 6
COURSE	SECTION	INSTRUCTOR	

1. Intercompany networking, also known as electronic data interchange (EDI), is a strategic advantage some companies have over their competitors. List two reasons why a company with EDI might have an advantage over a company without EDI capabilities. *Intercompany networking is the ability of separate information systems owned by different companies to communicate and share information with each other.*

■

■

2. Describe connectivity and its impact on the business community? Specifically, how does it relate to EDI? *This involves data communications on an anyone, anywhere, at-any-time basis.*

3. Why is a modem needed to transmit data over telephone lines? *The difference between digital and analog signals is important here.*

4. What is the value of special-function processors? *Think of the relationship between special-function processors and throughput.*

5. Multiplexers and front-end processors perform different functions, but they often work together to complete a data communications link. Describe how a down-line processor and a front-end processor work together to facilitate efficiency in data communications. *One feeds the other.*

6. Calculate how long would it take to send a file containing 256,000 bytes of data (each byte contains eight bits) over a communications channel with a capacity of 9.6k bps. *Divide the file size, in bits, by the channel capacity.*

7. Why is fiber optic cable not used in all data communications lines? *Cost is not the only reason.*

8. Where are earth-based microwave repeater stations positioned and why? If you have seen one, describe the terrain around its location. *Does the term "line-of-sight" mean anything here?*

9. Communications satellites are placed in geosynchronous orbits above the earth. What would the earth-based antennas have to do if the satellites were not in geosynchronous orbit? *You need to know what a goesynchronous orbit is to answer this question.*

10. If three satellites are theoretically enough to enable transmission of data throughout the world, why are there so many communications satellites in orbit? *The volume of communications transmissions and competition are improtant components of the answer to this question.*

11. Two common carriers, AT&T and Western Union, are mentioned in the text. Name two other telecommunications common carriers. *Several are heavily advertised on television.*

■

■

12. Under what circumstances would a private line be a better choice than a switched line for data communications? *How each line is priced in relation to the usage of the line are the central focus of this question.*

13. Examine the photos in Chapter 7 of the text. Describe the purpose for which data communications technology is being used in two of the photos. *Data communications can be across the world or to the desk sitting next to you. It can involve various types of channels from simple copper wires to sophisticated microwave relay networks.*

■

■

14. Name three types of LAN servers and discuss the functions of each. *These involve files and data, hardcopy output, and transferring data and information to various places.*

■

■

■

15. Briefly explain how a LAN operating system works. *LAN stands for local area network. Network topologies are important here also.*

16. Name two general classifications of communications protocols. Give an example application for each of these protocols. *See section 6-4 of the text.*

■

■

17. Describe the concept of digital convergence and its impact on our society. *The concept of digital convergence applies to both industries and products. See section 6-1 of the text.*

18. Discuss the purpose of a router in a computer network. *Think of a router in terms of communications protocols and a backbone. See section 6-2 of the text.*

19. Discuss the impact of wireless communications technology on the concepts of EDI and connectivity in the business community. *Have you thought about possible changes in the physical workplace, decentralization, work habits, productivity and productivity expectations, and competitive advantage, as well as its impact on hardware and software? See section 6-1 and section 6-3 of the text.*

20.   Compose a multiple-choice, a true/false, and an essay question that you think would be appropriate for a quiz on this chapter.

| *M/C:* |
| |
| (a) |
| (b) |
| (c) |
| (d) |
| *T/F:* |
| *Essay:* |

GRAPHICAL USER INTERFACE

Draw connecting lines between the computers pictured in each drawing below according to the network topologies indicated for each.

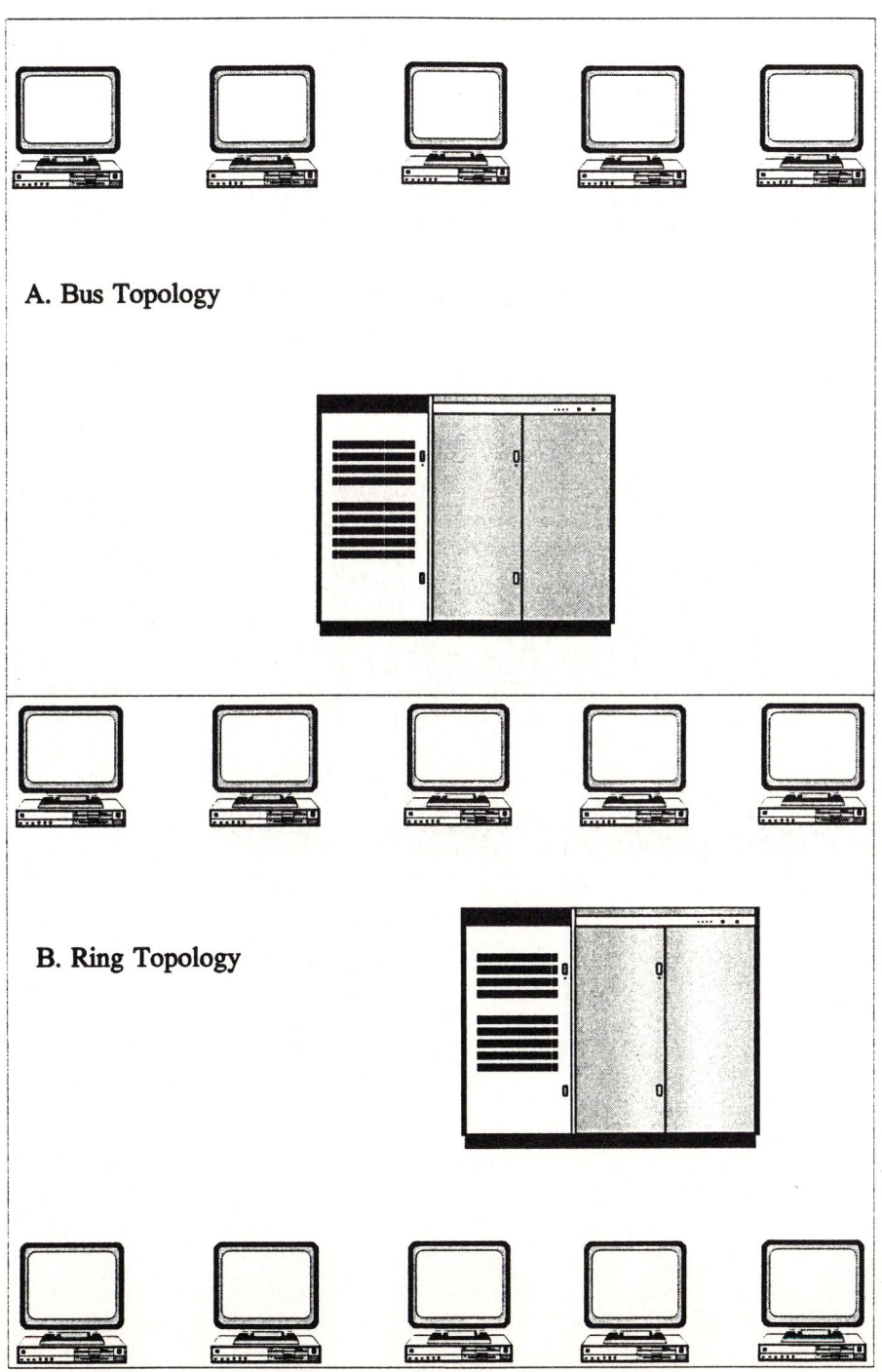

A. Bus Topology

B. Ring Topology

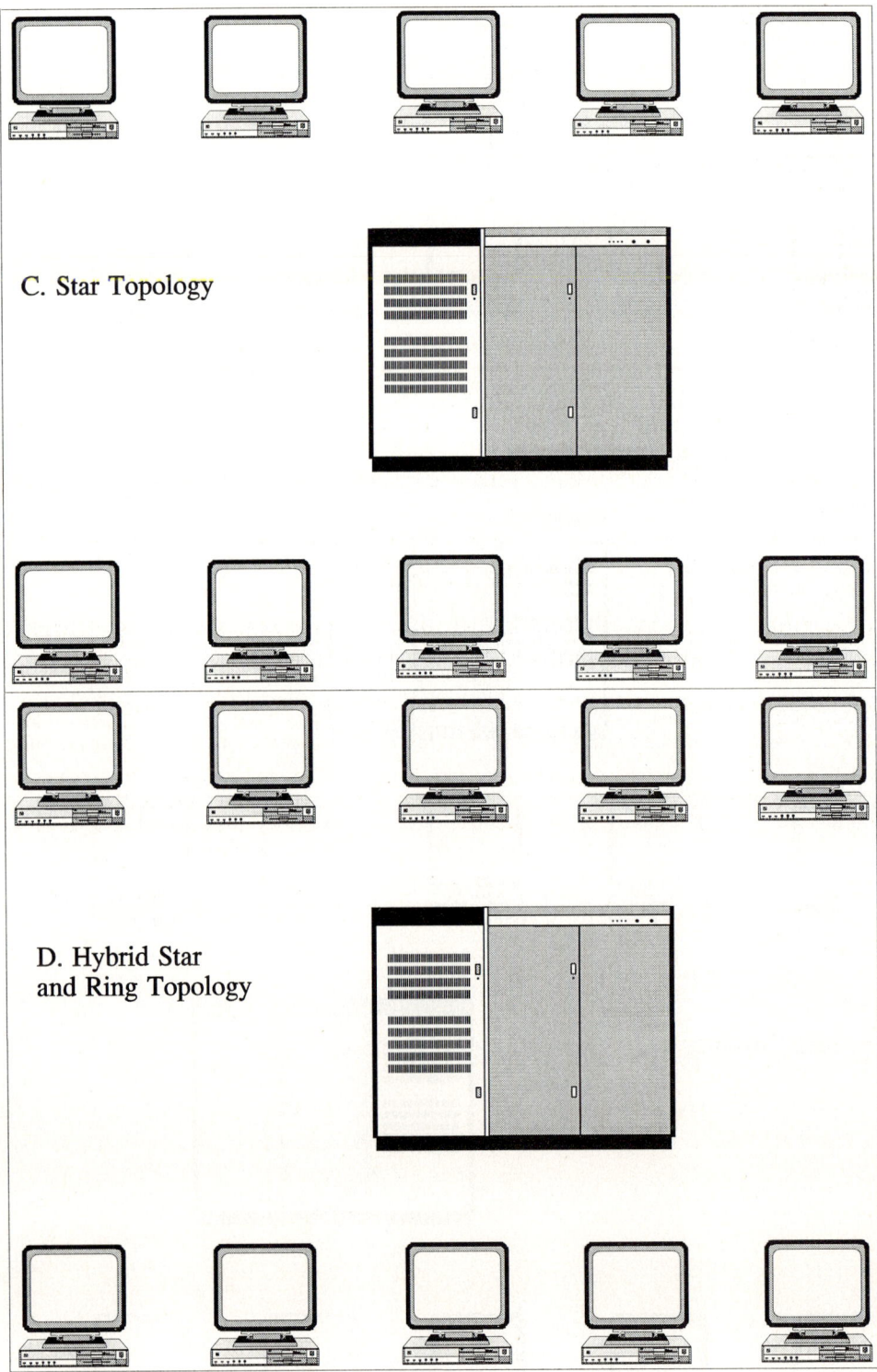

C. Star Topology

D. Hybrid Star
and Ring Topology

Chapter 7
Going On-line:
    Information Services,
the Net, and More

STUDENT LEARNING OBJECTIVES

■ To describe the purpose, use, and applications of general-purpose PC-based communications software.
■ To demonstrate an awareness of the scope of services made available by on-line information services (America Online, CompuServe, Prodigy, and so on).
■ To describe the Internet.
■ To demonstrate an awareness of the scope of services made available over the Internet.
■ To identify and describe common Internet capabilities.

VOCABULARY STUDY

anonymous FTP site
electronic funds transfer (EFT)
File Transfer Protocol (FTP)
full duplex
Gopher
half duplex
host mode
hypertext

information server
log off
log on
parity checking
password
system operator (sysop)
telecommuting
Telnet

terminal emulation mode
Transmission Control
Protocol/Internet Protocol
(TCP/IP)
WAIS
World Wide Web (the Web,
WWW, W3)

INTERACTIVE REVIEW

Use the terms in the Vocabulary Study to fill in the following blanks. You will only use each term once. You may need to insert a plural form of a term or adjust its verb tense. Check your answers with the chapter material and the glossary in your textbook.

7-1

The importance of communications software is pointed out by the fact that tens of millions of people are now _____ to work each day. Communications software provides the instructions which give a properly equipped PC access to the world by providing four basic functions. When a micro is in _____ _____ ____ , its keyboard, monitor, and data interface function like that of a terminal. The file transfer function enables the transfer of files between a micro and another computer. In ____ ____ operation, you can set up your PC so remote users can call in and establish a communications link via terminal emulation. Communications software is also used to send and receive faxes directly from your PC. When establishing a link with another computer, you must specify several data communications parameters, which may include specifying terminal type, file transfer protocol, and port settings which may include specifying the port used, the baud rate, _____ _____ (equal number of bits transmitted and received), data bits, stop bits, _____-_____ (one direction at a time), ____-_____ (both directions at once) data flow, echo, and perhaps others. Many communications software packages offer a communications profile and capture feature which can save a lot of time and headaches.

To interact with a remote computer, you must establish a link between your PC or terminal and the remote computer. The user must log on to the system once the link is made. The ___ __ procedure may require a _____ from the user to protect against unauthorized access. To terminate a session, the user must ___ ___ .

Data communications opens the door to a wealth of information and services. Along with information services such as Prodigy and America Online, there are electronic bulletin boards for virtually every profession, avocation, and interest. The person or group sponsoring a BBS is referred to as the _____ _____ or _____ .

7-2

More and more PC users are subscribing to commercial on-line information services, such as America Online, CompuServe, GEnie, Prodigy, Microsoft Network (MSN), e•World, The Source, Dow Jones News/Retrieval Service, DIALOG, and NewsNet. Still, less than 25% of PC owners subscribe to an on-line information service. To take advantage of these information services, you need a communications-equipped computer and a few dollars. You normally pay a one-time fee and a monthly service charge. For the initial fee, you get the communications software, a user ID and password, and a user's guide. Your monthly bill is based on how much you use the information service.

7-3

The Internet is the world's largest network and is comprised of thousands of independent networks at academic institutions, military installations, government agencies, commercial enterprises, and other organizations. In 1969, the Internet started operations as ARPANET with a link established between UCLA and Stanford University. Today, an estimated 50 million people a year use the Internet, and the number of Internet users is expected to reach 180 million by the year 2000. You can connect to the Internet via an information service such as Prodigy (an Internet service provider) or a direct network connection. Information services provide a necessary gateway to enable communication between the information service's native communications protocols and the Internet's _____ _____ _____/_____ _____ (___/__). The only way to get full Internet service via a dial-up connection is through an Internet service provider. Dial-up connections to a service provider are made through a SLIP (Serial Line Internet Protocol) or PPP (Point-to-Point Protocol) server on the service provider's Internet host. Interaction with the Internet is much faster through a direct network connection. To have a direct connection, your PC must be configured with TCP/IP software and be connected to a LAN that is linked to an Internet host. An Internet address consists of a user ID and a host/network identifier. The Internet address ends with either a country code for addresses outside the U. S. or an affiliation designation for U. S. addresses. There is an overwhelming number of applications available through the Net. Getting around the net can be simplified with any of a number of commercial and freeware software packages. Internet e-mail is available to and from anyone on the net. All that's needed is an address. Newsgroups (electronic discussion groups) and mailing lists abound on the net. Whatever you're interested in, you can probably find one of these applications that deals with it. You can use the _ _ _ _ _ _ _ _ _ _ _ _ _ _ _ _ _ _ _ (_ _ _) to download and upload files of all different kinds from the net. Tens of thousands of FTP sites offer millions of useful files, most are free for the asking. Some FTP sites require a password for access, but there are also many _ _ _ _ _ _ _ _ _ _ _ _ _ _ _ _ _ _ that maintain public archives. Many Internet sites use _ _ _ _ _ _ _ communications protocol that allows you to work from a PC as if it was a terminal linked directly to a host computer. Information is accessed on the net through an _ _ _ _ _ _ _ _ _ _ _ _ _ _ _ _ _ _ which is any Internet host with a repository of information that is made available over the Internet.

Searching the net for something can be like searching for a needle in a world-wide haystack. The three ways to search the Internet are search, browse, or ask someone. In searching the net, there are a variety of resource discovery tools to help you find the information or service you need. When you browse the Net you work through menu trees, selecting paths that meet your immediate information needs. People on the Net are a family, ready to help those in need. Don't hesitate to post an inquiry to a newsgroup or mailing list when you need help. One tool for finding information on the net is the _ _ _ _ _ _ system developed at University of Minnesota. The Gopher system is like a huge menu tree that allows you to keep choosing menu items until you find the information you want. _ _ _ _ offers another approach to information retrieval which allows you to search by content rather than poking around a hierarchy of menus to find the information you need. The two attributes that set the _ _ _ _ _ _ _ _ _ _ _ _ (also called _ _ _ _ _ _ , _ _ _ , and _ _) apart from other Internet servers are multimedia and _ _ _ _ _ _ _ _ _ . Growth of the WWW has been spectacular, due to a large extent to emergence of user-friendly Web browsers that take the mystery out of surfing the Internet. There are a number of commercial browsers available on the market that offer comprehensive functionality across Internet capabilities. Also, the commercial information services have created their own GUI tools for interacting with the Internet. A microsample of what you will find on the Internet includes the electronic newsstand, MUDers, love and war, the electronic confessional, travel information, subscription services, e-mail and geography. The Internet is just part of what is developing into the information superhighway. One day soon, we will be able to experience electronic family reunions, access unbelievable entertainment options, unlimited access to literature, transactions of all kinds using _ (_ _ _), instant personal communications of all kinds with friends all over the world, and perhaps even a cashless society and electronic voting.

As the settlers moved west, they brought law and order with them. It is doubtful that the Internet will remain unrestricted much longer. A small number of people forget that their freedom of speech also means others freedom to not have to listen. Another tiny group are malicious and have no respect for the property of others. Others find the actions of this tiny minority of renegades an opportunity to seize control of social institutions and force the imposition of their idea of regulation on everyone. The regulations that are adopted for the Internet depend entirely upon you. The will of the majority of only those who speak out to Congress will prevail. E-mail your opinions on Internet regulation to your senators and representative.

PRACTICE TEST

Multiple Choice *Circle the most appropriate answer.*

1.   The basic capabilities common to full-function communications packages include all of the following except
   a.   terminal emulsion.
   b.   file transfer.
   c.   host operation.
   d.   fax support.

2.   Zmodem, Xon/Xoff, and Kermit are examples of the
   a.   terminal emulation protocol.
   b.   file transfer protocol.
   c.   parity checking protocol.
   d.   data flow protocol.

3.   Determining that the number of bits transmitted equals the number of bits received is called
   a.   parity checking.
   b.   stop bit analysis.
   c.   baud rate.
   d.   party crashing.

4.   Most communications software packages allow the user to store communications parameters for various remote computer systems in a communications
   a.   protocol.
   b.   profile.
   c.   linker.
   d.   co-processor.

5.   Before completing the communications link with a remote computer, most log-on procedures require the user to enter a
   a.   passkey.
   b.   network address.
   c.   sysop designator.
   d.   password.

6.   The percentage of PC owners who subscribe to an on-line service is
   a.   less than 25%.
   b.   between 40% and 50%.
   c.   between 55% and 65%.
   d.   more than 75%.

7.   What we know today as the Internet was originally called
   a.   AARPNET.
   b.   ABBANET.
   c.   AIRNET.
   d.   ARPANET.

8.   The three basic ways to connect your PC to the Internet are via all of the following except
   a.   an information service.
   b.   a direct network connection.
   c.   a TCP/IP E-mail connection.
   d.   an Internet Service provider.

9.   The communications rules used for downloading and uploading files on the Internet are commonly referred to as
   a.   FAQ.   c.   FAT.
   b.   FPT.   d.   FTP.

10. An Internet system of information servers developed by the University of Minnesota is called
  a.   Mosaic.
  b.   Gopher.
  c.   Cello.
  d.   Netcom.

11. An Internet system of information servers that includes hypertext links is commonly referred to as
  a.   WWW.
  b.   WAIS.
  c.   WCS.
  d.   W4.

12. Using communications to go to work without physically going to another location is called
  a.   cyberworking.
  b.   telecommuting.
  c.   telecomputing.
  d.   electrocommuting.

True - False *Circle T for true and F for false.*

13. T F   A microcomputer can be converted to function as a terminal to a supercomputer through the use of terminal emulation software.

14. T F   A PC must use the host mode protocols provided by terminal emulation software to download files from a mainframe computer.

15. T F   To fax a word processing document with a PC, you must first print the document and then use a scanner to load the document into the PC fax software.

16. T F   XMODEM is a communications protocol.

17. T F   You use the data bits setting in communications software to specify the number of bits in the character or byte.

18. T F   Full duplex data flow transmits data in both directions, but only in one direction at a time.

19. T F   When echo is on during a data communications session between a micro and a host computer, the characters generated by the host computer appear on the micro's monitor.

20. T F   The use of passwords does not help protect a computer system.

21. T F   To establish a link with a mainframe computer, the micro user initiates the log-on procedure.

22. T F   Sysop is a term generally applied to the individual or group sponsoring a computer bulletin-board service.

23. T F   The official name of the Internet is the National Information Infrastructure.

24. T F   The first official demonstration of what eventually became the Internet linked UCLA with Stanford University.

25. T F   Communications over the net are built around the Transmission Protocol Control /Internet Communications (TPC/IC).

26. T F   A Point-to-Point Protocol server connection on an Internet service provider's Internet host is limited to phone line speeds.

27. T F   An Internet address consist of a user ID and a host/network identifier.

28. T F   The File Transfer Protocol (FTP) allows you to download and upload files on the Internet.

29. T F   Anonymous FTP sites on the Internet have been outlawed.

30. T F   An Internet service provider is an Internet host with a repository of information that is made available over the Internet.

Matching *Match the following terms with the appropriate definition or characteristic by placing the letter of the matching definition or characteristic in the blank.*

31.	_____ terminal emulation	(a)	An example of Internet browsing software
32.	_____host mode	(b)	Download and upload files on the Internet
33.	_____parity checking	(c)	Search the Internet by content
		(d)	Going to work via data communications
34.	_____ sysop	(e)	Internet information servers containing hypertext links
35.	_____ TCP/IP	(f)	Remote users call in and establish a communications link
36.	_____ FTP	(g)	Using data communications to transfer money from one account to another.
37.	_____Gopher	(h)	Ensures a transmission is complete and accurate
38.	_____ WAIS	(i)	Communications protocol required to connect to the Internet
39.	_____ WWW	(j)	ANSI, BBS, TTY, VT-100, VT-52, IBM 3270
40.	_____ spyglass	(k)	Bulletin-board system operator
		(l)	University of Minnesota
41.	_____ telecommuting		
42.	_____ EFT		

Answers to Practice Test **1** a, **2** b, **3** a, **4** b, **5** d, **6** a, **7** d, **8** c, **9** d, **10** b, **11** a, **12** b, **13** t, **14** f, **15** f, **16** t, **17** t, **18** f, **19** t, **20** f, **21** t, **22** t, **23** f, **24** t, **25** f, **26** f, **27** t, **28** t, **29** f, **30** f, **31** j, **32** f, **33** h, **34** k, **35** i, **36** b, **37** l, **38** c, **39** e, **40** a, **41** d, **42** g.

CHAPTER CHECKUP

NAME		DATE	CHAPTER 7
COURSE	SECTION	INSTRUCTOR	

1. Describe terminal emulation and its relationship to data communications. *This is basically the relationship between terminal emulation, the personal computer, the computer network, and the mainframe computer.*

2. Describe the fundamental differences between file transfer and terminal emulation data communications applications. *The level of interactivity available with each is a key factor.*

3. Describe both advantages and disadvantages of using a computer for faxing documents. *The other way to fax documents is to use a dedicated fax machine. See section 7-1 of the text.*

4. List five types of terminals that may be emulated by communications software. *To establish a link with a remote computer, your computer must emulate a terminal that is accepted by the host. Most host systems will hook up with several popular types of terminals. See section 7-1 of the text.*

-
-
-
-
-

5. List four file transfer protocols that may be available with communications software. *These protocols are the rules used by the two computer systems for copying data from the secondary storage of one linked computer to the secondary storage in another. See section 7-1 of the text.*

-
-
-
-

6. List and describe five parameters you may be required to specify to establish a link with another computer. *This is analogous to being sure that everyone in a musical combo is using the same musical score and will be playing in the same key at the same tempo.*

-
-
-
-
-

7. What is the difference between full-duplex and half-duplex data communications? *This is similar to a two-way radio verses a telephone. See section 7-1 of the text.*

8. Describe the differences between a bulletin-board system and a commercial on-line information service. *Examples of commercial on-line information services include America Online, CompuServe, GEnie, Prodigy, Microsoft Network (MSN), e^GWorld, The Source, Dow Jones News/Retrieval Service, DIALOG, and NewsNet. See section 7-1 of the text.*

9. List five commercial on-line information services available to the general public. *Start with CompuServe.*

-
-
-
-
-

10. What was the original name of the Internet? What government agency developed it and describe its first official demonstration. *The government agency was a part of the Department of Defense, and the first official demonstration took place the same year Neil Armstrong walked on the Moon and Country Joe and the Fish played at Woodstock. See section 7-3 of the text.*

11. Describe the three basic ways to connect your PC to the Internet. *Prodigy or your school's or employer's computer system may be involved in two of the ways. See section 7-3 of the text.*

■

■

■

12. Give an example of an Internet address and describe its various components. *Addresses located in countries other than the U. S. are different than U. S addresses. See section 7-3 of the text.*

13. Compare and contrast an Internet newsgroup, an Internet mailing list and Internet e-mail. *All three have distinct similarities such as addresses and accessability, and differences such as who sends what information where and when. See section 7-3 of the text.*

14. In relation to the Internet, what does FTP stand for and what is it used for? *FTP is important for copying information from an Internet source to secondary storage on your computer. See section 7-3 of the text.*

15. Describe three major types of information servers on the Internet and what are the differences between them. *See section 7-3 of the text.*

■

■

■

16. List five different examples of software that can be used for browsing the Internet. *One was developed by the National Center for Supercomputer Applications, and is distributed free of charge. See section 7-3 of the text.*

-

-

-

-

-

17. Describe a separate example for each of the following available over the Internet. *Periodicals, games, personal communications, religion, and education are just a few examples of subjects that can be used. See section 7-3 of the text.*

(a.)   applications

(b.)   retrievable files

(c.)   communication services

(d.)   information services

18. List two advantages and two disadvantages of telecommuting. *Versitility and control are important matters here. See section 7-4 of the text.*

Advantages:
-

-

Disadvantages:
-

-

19. Do you expect the number of telecommuters to increase or decrease in the future? Why? *An understanding of the term telecommuting and its various components and uses is a key factor to this question. See section 7-4 of the text.*

20. Compose a multiple-choice, a true/false, and an essay question that you think would be appropriate for a quiz on this chapter.

M/C:
(a)
(b)
(c)
(d)
T/F:
Essay:

GRAPHICAL USER INTERFACE

Match the appropriate America Online service for each item in the table below.

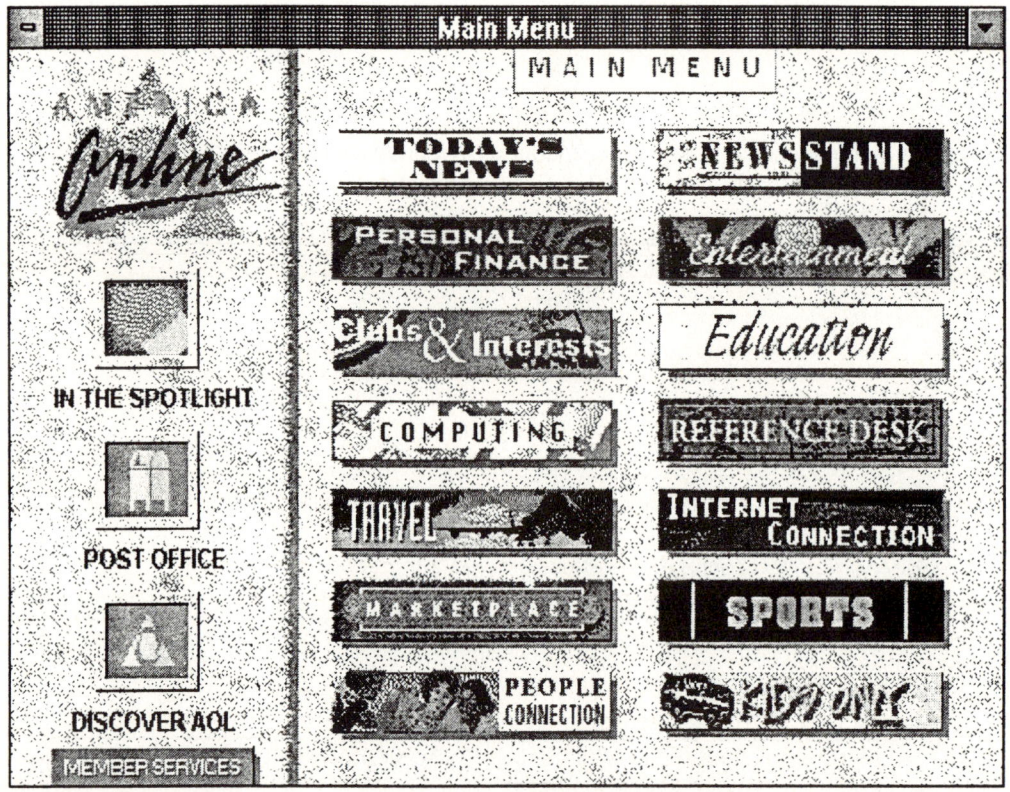

1.	Time Magazine		9.	Courses On-line	
2.	World Wide Web		10.	Reuters Hourly News Service	
3.	Shareware downloads		11.	Compton's Encyclopedia	
4.	NFL scores		12.	Bicycling Magazine	
5.	E-mail		13.	On-line chats	
6.	Nintendo Power Source		14.	Finance Forums	
7.	Movie reviews		15.	Downtown AOL	
8.	EAAsy Sabre				

Chapter 8
Productivity Software:
 From Notes to Databases

STUDENT LEARNING OBJECTIVES

- To describe the function and applications of word processing software.
- To understand word processing concepts.
- To describe the function and applications of desktop publishing software.
- To understand desktop publishing concepts.
- To describe and illustrate the relationships between the levels of the hierarchy of data organization.
- To describe the function and applications of spreadsheet software.
- To understand common spreadsheet concepts.
- To describe the function and applications of database software.
- To understand common database software concepts.
- To describe the concepts associated with programming and programs.

VOCABULARY STUDY

arithmetic operators	flat file	pointer
boilerplate	font	query by example
cell	frame	ranges
cell address	full-screen editing	relational database
clip art	grammar and style checker	relational operator
database	insert mode	spelling checker
DTP (desktop publishing)	key field	typefaces
electronic dictionary	logical operators	typeover mode
field	online thesaurus	WYSIWYG

INTERACTIVE REVIEW

Use the terms in the Vocabulary Study to fill in the following blanks. You will only use each term once. You may need to insert a plural form of a term or adjust its verb tense. Check your answers with the chapter material and the glossary in your textbook.

8-1&2

Writing is made much simpler and faster with computers and text software. Today, word processing is the standard operating procedure for business correspondence activities and a considerable amount of personal correspondence. Word processing allows you to not only create original documents but also to recall an existing document from disk storage for editing and printing. Document formatting is simple and easy with a word processor, and once a common format is established, it can be saved as default settings. This saves considerable time when creating new documents. Text is entered in either _ _ _ _ _ _ _ _ _ _ _ or _ _ _ _ _ _ _ _ _ _ _ _ . You can move the cursor to any position in a document with the _ _ _ _ - _ _ _ _ _ _ _ _ _ _ _ _ _ feature and you can browse through a multiscreen document by scrolling a line, screen, or page at a time. The _ _ _ _ _ _ _ _ feature generally allows you to view your document on the screen essentially as it will be printed on paper. This is important for checking such things as the _ _ _ _ (size and style of typeface) and graphics in your document. Most modern word processing packages are considered WYSIWYG. In most older word processing packages, you can look while in this mode, but you cannot edit.

The block feature enables the electronic equivalent of a cut and paste job on a document. Blocked text is usually displayed in reverse video and can be copied to the clipboard, a temporary storage area in RAM, where it can be recalled and inserted into the same or many other types of documents. The find features allow you to locate a specific letter, symbol, command, word, or string within a document. The find-and-replace feature allows you to locate the search string and automatically replace it with a new string.

Virtually all word processing packages have additional features that can be used to enhance the appearance and readability of documents. Some of these features may include centering, boldface, underline, left and right justification, indent, header and footer labels, pagination, hyphenation, footnoting, numbered list, outline, bulleted list, line-draw, superscript, subscript, image insert, and multicolumn output. Most packages even allow you to mix fonts within a single document. The more sophisticated word processing packages can automatically produce a table of contents and a list of key words, and have a table feature which expedites the tabular presentation of data. The best word processing packages even provide desktop publishing features. The more sophisticated the package, the more flexibility there is for printing documents and interfacing with communications software and hardware to fax documents. Once a document is completed, it can be saved to disk storage. The file feature of word processing packages allows you to at least save, retrieve, and delete these files, and more sophisticated packages provide even more file manipulation features.

Add-on features available for most word processing packages are often bundled with the package when it is purchased. A package called an _ _ - _ _ _ _ _ _ _ _ _ _ _ _ _ provides lists of alternative words with similar meanings. A _ _ _ _ _ _ _ _ _ _ _ _ _ _ _ _ will identify spelling errors by comparing each word to an _ . A _ highlights grammatical concerns and deviations from conventions.

Word processing can be used to enhance and streamline many business operations. A good example of this is the mail-merge feature available on some word processing packages which allows a document to be combined with parts of a database to create multiple personalized letters from a single document. Also, a substantial amount of keyboarding can be eliminated by simply modifying a _ _ _ _ _ _ _ _ _ _ _ (existing text) to create customized documents. Another time saver provided by most state-of-the-art word processing packages is the integration of text and graphic images into a single document. Some word processing packages allow you to establish hypertext links in documents. These let you you tie parts of a document or different documents together. Hypertext links make it easy to skip around a document to find what you want.

By using a word processing package, you can minimize the effort you must devote to the routine aspects of writing and focus your attention on its creative aspects. Your finished product will be less verbose, better organized, devoid of spelling errors, and, of course, more visually appealing.

8-3

Desktop publishing, or _ _ _ as it is sometimes abbreviated, refers to the capability of producing near-typeset-quality camera copy from the confines of a desktop. While word processing software is designed to manipulate words in a document, DTP software is designed to manipulate all of the various objects that make up a document. The quality of the DTP-produced camera-ready copy is dependent on the quality of available input and output devices. The components required for desktop publishing include document-composition software, microcomputer, desktop page printer, image scanner, typefaces and fonts, clip art and illustration software. Document-composition software is combined with a high-end microcomputer to enable users to design and make up the page or pages of a document. A DTP document will involve one or more text files, perhaps one or more picture files, a style-sheet file, and a print file. The document-composition process with DTP consists of the following four steps: preparing text and graphics, creating the style sheet, combining text and picture files, and printing the document. Desktop page printers with resolutions from 300 dpi to 2000 dpi or higher are used for hardcopy output. Image scanners are used to digitize images, such as photographs. The various fonts used in documents can be built from a variety of _ _ _ _ _ _ _ _ _ . A typeface refers to a set of characters of the same type style while a font is described by its typeface, its height in points and its presentation attribute. _ _ _ _ _ _ _ , prepackaged electronic images that are stored on disk, is often used to enhance document appearance. One of the handiest features of desktop publishing software is the clip art browser. An illustration program (paint or draw software) is nice to have if you intend to create original illustrations for inclusion in a DTP document. A typical DTP-produced document consists of several files. During the document-composition process, each file or resource is assigned to a rectangular _ _ _ _ _ _ . Full scale DTP requires the integration of word processing with DTP software. Word processing packages simply do not offer the flexibility in formatting documents that is achieved by DTP at this time. However, the distinctions between the two become more blurred with the introduction of each new generation of word processing and DTP software.

8-4

Familiarity with the terms and concepts associated with the hierarchy of data organization and database management systems is important if one is to learn the principles of data management software. The hierarchy of data organization has six levels. Bits are represented by 1s and 0s that are combined to represent a character called a byte. Bytes are combined to create a _ _ _ _ _ which is the lowest level logical unit in the data hierarchy. Related fields describing an event or item are logically grouped to form a record. The record is also the lowest level logical unit that can be accessed from a file. A file is a collection of related records. It can also be a named area on a secondary storage device that contains a program, textual material, or an image. Files are manipulated and processed by a _ _ _ _ _ _ _ _ _ . A file is said to be a _ _ _ _ _ _ _ _ when it does not point to or physically link with another file. The _ _ _ _ _ _ _ _ is the data resource for every computer-based information system. It is a collection of files that are in some way logically related to one another with data redundancy minimized.

8-5

Spreadsheet software is an electronic alternative to thousands of traditionally manual tasks. The primary difference between spreadsheet packages is in the user interface. All enable the user to manipulate rows and columns of data. A spreadsheet model that contains the layout and formulas needed to produce an often repeated spreadsheet operation is called a template. Larger spreadsheets require the user to scroll the VDT display screen up, down, left, and right to view all elements of the spreadsheet. The intersection of a row and column in the tabular structure of a spreadsheet is called a _ _ _ _ . Most spreadsheet packages will number the rows and identify each column with a letter. A _ _ _ _ _ _ _ _ _ _ identifies the location of a cell in the spreadsheet by its column and row. The highlighted area that identifies the current cell is called the _ _ _ _ _ _ _ _ , and must be positioned at the particular cell to which data are to be added or edited. The address, content, and other information of the current cell are displayed in the user-interface portion of the spreadsheet called the cell status line. A cell can be

formatted to automatically display data in a particular form such as a date or as currency. The four types of _____ are cell, column, row, and block, and are identified by the addresses of opposing corners or endpoint cells. Cell entries are classified as either label, numeric, formula, or date/time. Label entries are any string of alphanumeric text. Numeric entries are only numbers. A formula enables the spreadsheet software to perform numeric and/or string calculations and/or logic operations that result in either a numeric value or an alphanumeric character string. Formulas use standard notation for
_____ _____ . Judicious use of the formatting options provided by spreadsheet packages can greatly enhance the appearance and readability of your spreadsheets.

Most spreadsheet software is actually part of an integrated package that also includes presentation graphics, and database capabilities. The graphics component enables users to present spreadsheet data as business graphs such as bar graphs, stacked-bar graphs, cluster-bar graphs, pie graphs, exploded-pie graphs, line graphs, and others.

8-6

All database software packages provide the user with the capability to create and maintain a database, extract and list all records or only those records that meet certain conditions, make an inquiry, sort records in ascending or descending sequence by primary, secondary, and tertiary fields, and to generate formatted reports with subtotals and totals. The more sophisticated packages include a variety of other features, such as spreadsheet-type computations, presentation graphics, and programming. In a typical database, related fields are grouped to form records.

The relational approach to database management organizes data into tables in which a row is equivalent to a record. One or more tables comprise a database or file, as it is often called. The user defines a database structure by identifying the name, type, and size for each field. A
_____ _____ accesses data by content rather than by address. The best way to enter data is to establish a screen format that permits convenient data entry. In retrieving, viewing, and printing records with _____ __ _____ (___), the user composes one or more example relational expressions. A relational expression normally compares one or more field names to numbers or character strings using one or more of the _____ _____ such as =, >, and <. Also, several conditions can be combined with _____ _____ such as AND, OR, and NOT. Inquiries to the database also can be made for a display of calculated information.

To sort records within a database, the user identifies the key field by which to sort the records. Most database packages allow sorting to be conducted using several key fields arranged in a hierarchy. In this case, the user defines the primary, secondary, and tertiary key fields as needed. Database software allows the user to design the layout for and create customized, or formatted, reports. The user describes the layout of the customized report interactively, then stores it for later use in what is usually called a report file. Users can generate sophisticated reports that involve subtotals, calculations, presentation graphics, and programming.

PRACTICE TEST

Multiple Choice *Circle the most appropriate answer.*

1. Which of the following is not normally associated with word processing?
    a. full-screen editing
    b. pagination
    c. block operations
    d. query by example

2. A spreadsheet model is commonly referred to as a
    a. pointer.
    b. template.
    c. operator.
    d. mask.

3. To be in typeover mode in word processing means that
    a. the text you enter overstrikes the character at the cursor position.
    b. you have full-screen editing possibilities.
    c. the layout line is defined.
    d. the text you enter is inserted at the cursor position.

4. In query by example, you set conditions for the selection of records by composing one or more example
    a. structure components.
    b. logical expressions.
    c. screen formats.
    d. relational expressions.

5. The basic components required for minimal desktop publishing are the
    a. word processing software and a PC.
    b. desktop publishing software and a dot matrix printer.
    c. document composition and font software, a micro, and a page printer.
    d. micro and a daisywheel printer.

6. Which of the following represents a block range as opposed to a row or column range?
    a. B6..D8
    b. B12..B45
    c. B2..D2
    d. A17..A20

7. Existing images that are stored on disk and used for enhancing documents are called
    a. clip art.
    b. clip images.
    c. boilerplates.
    d. photo clips.

8. Which of the following terms is normally associated with DTP?
    a. boilerplate
    b. frame
    c. mail-merge
    d. idea processor

9. Which of the following would not normally be used with a microcomputer to produce camera-ready copy for desktop publishing?
    a. an image scanner
    b. DTP software
    c. impact printer
    d. clip art

10.   Which of the following is not considered a relational operator?
        a.   ,
        b.   >
        c.   <>
        d.   =
11.   Existing text that can be accessed and customized for a variety of circumstances is called a
        a.   template.
        b.   boilerplate.
        c.   frameplate.
        d.   dinnerplate.
12.   Sorting a database table requires the selection of a
        a.   logical operator.
        b.   query structure.
        c.   key field.
        d.   relational operator.

True - False   *Circle T for true and F for false.*

13.   T F   WYSIWYG is an acronym meaning what you see on the screen is what the document will look like when it is printed.
14.   T F   When text is entered in insert mode, it overstrikes existing text.
15.   T F   Formatting a document entails describing the page size and how you want the document to look when it is printed.
16.   T F   Insert mode is used to line up the text on the right margin.
17.   T F   Text generated by word processing can be merged with data from a database.
18.   T F   Idea processors are also called operating systems.
19.   T F   A typeface refers to a set of characters that are of the same type style.
20.   T F   The quality of DTP documents produced by desktop page printers is between 1200 and 4200 dpi.
21.   T F   A spelling checker is normally used to locate punctuation errors in a word processing document.
22.   T F   A record is the lowest level logical unit in the data hierarchy.
23.   T F   A spreadsheet is a tabular structure made up of rows and columns.
24.   T F   In spreadsheets, data are referenced by their network address.
25.   T F   Selecting records by setting conditions is sometimes called query by example.
26.   T F   Databases can be sorted using a primary and secondary key field.
27.   T F   Before entering records into a database for the first time, you must set up the structure of the database.
28.   T F   Logical and relational operators are not used in database software.
29.   T F   In spreadsheets, data are referenced by their network address.
30.   T F   In a spreadsheet, the ranges C3..F9 and C9..F3 refer to the same cells.

Matching *Match the following terms with the appropriate definition or characteristic by placing the letter of the matching definition or characteristic in the blank.*

31. ____ spreadsheet	(a) The fifth level in the hierarchy of data and consists of a collection of related records.
32. ____logical operators	(b) Indicates the location of the current cell in spreadsheet software
33. ____relational operator	(c) Adding a character to a word processing document without erasing existing text
34. ____ typeface	(d) Setting conditions for the selection of records by composing the equality relationship between two expressions.
35. ____ database software	(e) Software that combines spreadsheet, presentation graphics, and database capabilities
36. ____ full-screen editing	(f) Tool for working with rows and columns of data
37. ____insert mode	(g) Holds the text or image of a particular file in a DTP document
38. ____ frame	(h) Text cursor can be moved to any position to insert or typeover text
39. ____ integrated package	(i) Used in spreadsheet and database formulas to show one or more examples of relational expressions
40. ____ file	(j) The term that refers to the software that manages the database
41. ____ pointer	(k) AND, OR
42. ____ query by example	(l) Set of characters that are the same style

Answers to Practice Test **1** d, **2** b, **3** a, **4** d, **5** c, **6** a, **7** a, **8** b, **9** c, **10** a, **11** b, **12** c, **13** t, **14** f, **15** t, **16** f, **17** t, **18** f, **19** t, **20** f, **21** f, **22** f, **23** t, **24** f, **25** t, **26** t, **27** t, **28** f, **29** f, **30** t, **31** f, **32** k, **33** i, **34** l, **35** j, **36** h, **37** c, **38** g, **39** e, **40** a, **41** b, **42** d.

CHAPTER CHECKUP

NAME		DATE	CHAPTER 8
COURSE	SECTION	INSTRUCTOR	

1. Give two examples of default format settings for a word processing document? *There are many default settings in a word processor. Not all are format settings, however. See section 8-2 of the text.*

■

■

2. How does typeover mode differ from insert mode? *See section 8-2 of the text.*

3. What does the acronym WYSIWYG mean and how is this helpful in word processing software? *Each letter of the term WYSIWYG stands for another word. See section 8-2 of the text.*

4. What are hypertext links? Why and how would you use them in a document? *See section 8-2 of the text.*

5. Describe a mail-merge application relating to your major or profession. *See section 8-2 of the text.*

6. In reference to word processing, what is a boilerplate? Give an example of how one could be used with the mail-merge feature of a word processor to enhance productivity in a business setting. *A boilerplate in this context is a software item that can be used to produce customized hardcopy. See section 8-2 of the text.*

7. Modern word processing programs offer a variety of helpful writing tools that you can use to help improve your writing and check your document for errors. Select three of these tools listed in the text or with which you are familiar. Describe how each would be used in business correspondence. *PC add-ins include a spelling checker, an on-line Thesaurus, a style and grammar checker, and many others. See section 8-2 of the text.*

■

■

■

8. Why do you think desktop publishing has become so popular? *How can it save individuals and companies a lot of money? See section 8-3 of the text.*

9. Name five common components of a desktop publishing system. *There are a total of seven. See section 8-3 of the text.*

■

■

■

■

■

10. A DTP-produced document is generated from several different files. Name and describe two desktop publishing files. *There is a total of four. See section 8-3 of the text.*

■

■

11. Under what circumstances would someone opt to use DTP over word processing software? *While the line between DTP and WP is getting more blurred every day, there is still a significant difference between the two types of software. See section 8-3 of the text.*

12. List the six levels of the hierarchy of data organization and give a brief description of each. *See section 8-4 of the text.*

■

■

■

■

■

■

13. List the four types of ranges shown in Figure 8-10 of the text and define each using cell addresses. *The highlighted range has a heavy or thick red border around them. An example of a range defined by cell address would be B3..D6. See section 8-5 of the text.*

■

■

■

■

14. Explain the difference between numeric and formula cell entries. *See section 8-5 of the text.*

15. In the stacked-bar graph of Figure 8-13 in the text, which region sold the most CROWN? The least number of MONARCH? *Individual item comparisons with stacked bar charts can be tricky and difficult to read. Pay close attention to the height of each section individually, not as they are stacked on top of each other. See section 8-5 of the text.*

16. What must be specified when defining the structure of a database? *See section 8-6 of the text.*

17. Give three examples of relational operators and three examples of logical operators. *See section 8-6 of the text.*

Relational Operators:
-

-

-

Logical Operators:
-

-

-

18. In Figure 8-15 in the text book, the field type and size for TITLE is A20. What does the A and the 20 indicate? Be specific. *This refers to parameters or definition, not addresses or locations. See section 8-6 of the text.*

    A --

    20 --

19. Look at the COURSE table in Figure 8-14 in the text. If TITLE is the primary key field and the database is sorted in ascending order, what would be the rank of WordPerfect, MIS Orientation, Lotus 1-2-3, and business COBOL? *Wouldn't this be some sort of alphabetical order? See section 8-6 of the text.*

WordPerfect

MIS Orientation

Lotus 1-2-3

business COBOL

20. Compose a multiple-choice, a true/false, and an essay question that you think would be appropriate for a quiz on this chapter.

M/C:

       (a)

       (b)

       (c)

       (d)

T/F:

Essay:

GRAPHICAL USER INTERFACE

Match each description in 1–9 with the letter for the appropriate spreadsheet item(s) shown below.
(Some items may apply to more than one description).

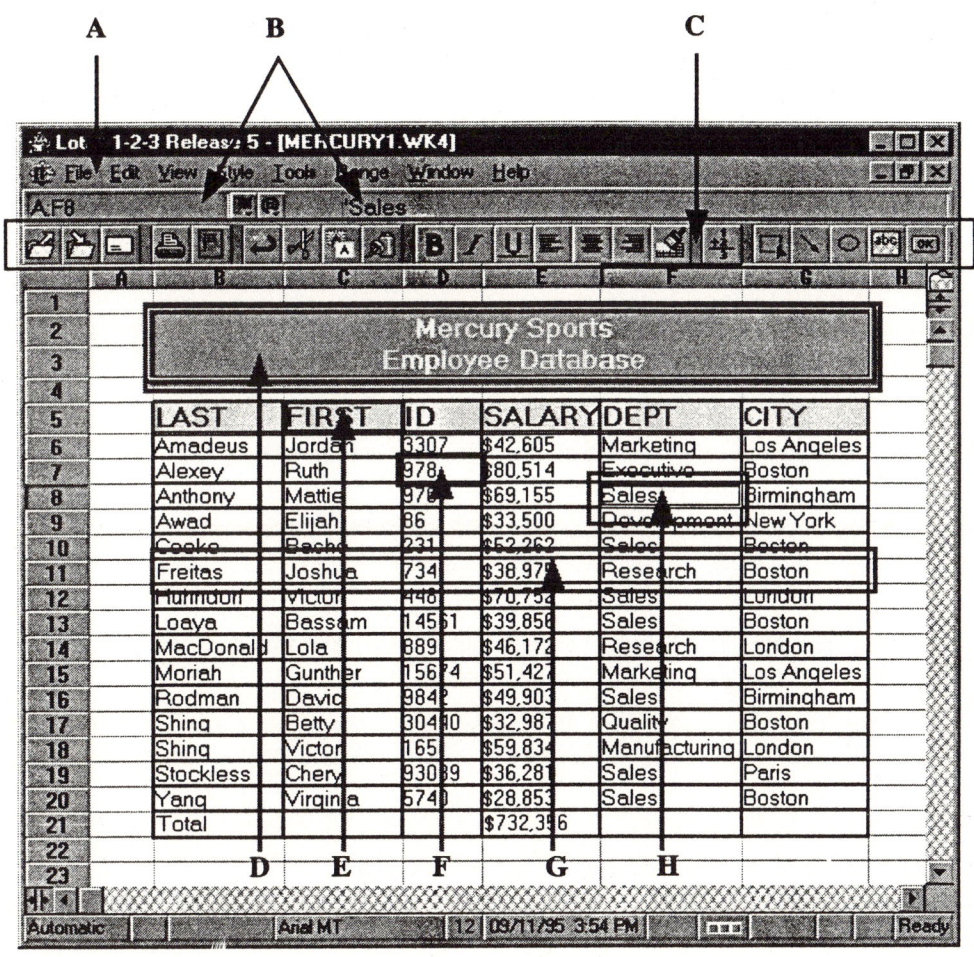

1.	_____	Label field
2.	_____	Current cell status and contents
3.	_____	Bar menu
4.	_____	Numeric field
5.	_____	Record
6.	_____	Current cell
7.	_____	Alpha field
8.	_____	Button bar
9.	_____	Row

Refer to the spreadsheet on the previous page to answer questions 10–15.

10.   What is the cell address of the current cell?

11.   What is the cell address of the cell most likely to contain a formula?

       a.   Write a formula for this cell without using functions.

       b.   Write a formula for this cell using functions.

12.   What is the range of cells which would require new entries each month?

13.   What are the ranges of cells with contents (not display) that would remain constant each month? (Assume no personnel or location changes.)

14.   Identify the field on which the records in the display are sorted.

15.   Identify the largest range in this display which contains only cells formatted for currency.

Chapter 9
Graphics and Multimedia:
Tickling Our Senses

STUDENT LEARNING OBJECTIVES

- To understand graphics software concepts.
- To describe the functions of different types of graphics software.
- To understand multimedia concepts and applications.
- To identify hardware and software associated with multimedia.
- To describe the functions of different types of software associated with multimedia.

VOCABULARY STUDY

animation
authoring software
bar graph
bit-mapped
draw software
metafile

MIDI file
morphing
multimedia upgrade kit
paint software
photo illustration software
pie graph

raster graphics
software suite
vector graphics
wave file

INTERACTIVE REVIEW

Use the terms in the Vocabulary Study to fill in the following blanks. You will only use each term once. You may need to insert a plural form of a term or adjust its verb tense. Check your answers with the chapter text and glossary in the textbook.

9-1

　　　　If you wish to add pizzazz to documents produced with basic software products, you will want to familiarize yourself with graphics and multimedia software. That pizzazz could be anything from colorful illustrations to full multimedia presentations involving sound, animation, and motion video.

9-2

　　　　Graphic software facilitates the creation and management of computer-based images. The six dominant categories of graphics software are paint, draw, drag-and-drop, presentation graphics, animation, and screen capture and graphics conversion. Images produced by _ _ _ _ _ _ _ _ _ _ _ _ _ _ are composed of picture elements or pixels and are often called _ _ _ - _ _ _ _ _ _ images. _ _ _ _ _ _ _ _ _ _ _ _ _ _ _ are used to produce images composed of patterns of lines, points, and other geometric shapes. _ _ _ _ _ _ _ _ _ store images by combining components of raster and vector graphics formats.

　　　　The six items in the typical user interface provided by a typical _ _ _ _ _ _ _ _ _ _ _ _ _ package are the drawing area, graphics cursor, main menu, tool box, linesize box, and color palette. Raster graphics are used by this software to create images. You must erase or draw over any part of a paint software drawing with which you are dissatisfied.

　　　　The use of vector graphics by _ _ _ _ _ _ _ _ _ _ _ _ provides for greater flexibility in manipulating images than is possible with raster graphics. A specific object can be moved, copied, deleted, rotated, tilted, flipped horizontally or vertically, stretched, and squeezed. Artists will often use conversion programs to create templates from bitmapped images that can be the basis for original vector artwork. A user can create a wide variety of visually appealing and informative presentation enhancements such as range bar charts, scatter diagrams, _ _ _ _ _ _ _ _ _ , _ _ _ _ _ _ _ _ _ , and other types of graphs and charts complete with annotated titles, labels, and legends in a matter of seconds with the use of _ . In addition to traditional business graphs, many presentation graphics software packages provide the user with the ability to prepare text charts, organization charts, and maps. Besides offering the ability to prepare graphs and charts from user-supplied data, some presentation graphics packages let you create and store original drawings. Recent editions of graphics software can even replace the traditional slide presentation with a dynamic show with visually interesting transition between the various slides such as fading out.

　　　　Movement of images, or _ _ _ _ _ _ _ _ _ , is accomplished by the rapid repositioning (moving) of an area of the screen. Some animation features that may be used in a presentation include animated bullet build and animated charting. Today's high-performance micros can be configured with very high-resolution large-screen monitors, a variety of pointing and drawing devices, plotters, and whatever else is needed to use sophisticated imaging software. Computer graphics are finding their way into virtually every subject and profession imaginable.

9-3

　　　　Most computer experts agree that multimedia refers to a computer system that lets users access and interact with computer-based text, high-resolution still graphics, motion visuals, animation, and sound. Three elements in particular distinguish multimedia: sound, motion, and the opportunity for interaction. To enjoy the full range of the multimedia computer experience, you need a 386 (or better) PC or its equivalent equipped with a high-resolution monitor, a CD-ROM drive, a sound card, external speakers, and a microphone. With that, you will be ready to take advantage of multimedia support software and multimedia applications software.

　　　　Starter multimedia software would normally include that which is distributed with the sound card or operating system. Multimedia support software includes sound assembly programs, text to speech synthesizer software, and _ _ _ _ _ _ _ _ _ _ _ _ _ _ _ _ _ that lets you create multimedia applications that integrate sound, motion, text, animation, and images.

If your PC is not currently equipped for multimedia, you can purchase a _ _ _ _ _ _ _ _ _ _ _ _ _ _ _ _ _ _ _ that includes the hardware and software necessary to launch you into the world of multimedia computing. As you gain proficiency with multimedia, you may want to add a Video camera, videocassette recorder/player, audiocassette player, CD-audio player, television, synthesizer, video capture card, color scanner, applications development software, and source libraries to your computing inventory.

Multimedia applications draw content material from a number of sources. These sources include text files, database files, sound files, image files, animation files, and motion video files. There are two types off sound files. The _ _ _ _ _ _ _ _ consists of the digital information needed to reconstruct the analog waveform of the sound so it can be played through speakers. Non-waveform files such as the _ _ _ _ _ _ _ _ , contain instructions as to how to create the sound, rather than a digitized version of the actual sound. Image files may contain user created images, clip art, scanned images, and photo images. Multimedia applications come in all shapes and sizes, and with the right tools, you can create your own multimedia applications to fit your own special needs. Multimedia possibilities stretch the human imagination to its limits. Multimedia applications touch our lives no matter which way we turn and what we can do in the future boggles the mind.

9-4

During the last few years, major software vendors have been creating and pushing _ _ _ _ _ _ _ _ _ _ _ _ _ _ which include, to varying degrees, most of the major business applications packages or capabilities such as communications, word processing, desktop publishing, spreadsheet, database, graphics, and multimedia. The various programs within a given software suite have a common interface and are integrated for easy transfer of information among programs. A suite may cost as little as 30% to 50% of the cost of the individually priced programs. Each suite has its advantages and disadvantages, so investigate thoroughly and choose carefully when considering the value of one of these packages.

PRACTICE TEST

Multiple Choice *Circle the letter of the most appropriate answer.*

1. Which of the following terms is not associated with the fundamental operation of raster graphics?
   a. picture element
   b. pixel
   c. geometric shape
   d. bit-mapped
2. Which of the following is not a common capability of graphics software?
   a. paint software
   b. presentation graphics software
   c. animation
   d. desktop publishing
3. Which of the following defines images as individual geometric shapes?
   a. paint software
   b. vector graphics
   c. wave software
   d. raster graphics
4. Images are stored as a combination of raster graphics and vector graphics in
   a. MIDI files.   c. wave files.
   b. metafiles.   d. document files.

5. Which of the following hardware items is not specifically associated with a multimedia computer system?
   a. multiplexer
   b. microphone
   c. external speakers
   d. CD-ROM drive

6. Which type of software enables the integration of data, text, graphics, sounds, and full-motion video?
   a. cartoon
   b. database
   c. spreadsheet
   d. multimedia

7. Special effects sounds and simulated musical instrument sounds are produced with
   a. an XMODEM.
   b. a multiplexer.
   c. a synthesizer.
   d. a sysop.

8. Showing the changes that take place as one image is modified to become an entirely different image is called
   a. vectoring.
   b. animation.
   c. charting.
   d. morphing.

9. The automatic display of a series of slides on a computer is an important capability of
   a. presentation software.
   b. animation software.
   c. multimedia support software.
   d. metafile software.

10. A MIDI file is considered to be a
    a. wave file.
    b. non-waveform file.
    c. clip file.
    d. wavefrom file.

11. Each of the following types of files are classified as image files except
    a. clip art.
    b. photo images.
    c. video clip imaging.
    d. scanned images.

12. Microsoft Office Professional and PerfectOffice from Novell are referred to as
    a. software jackets.
    b. software offices.
    c. software works.
    d. software suites.

True - False *Circle T next to each true statement and F next to each false statement.*

13. T F Paint software permits the user to selectively change one color for another within a user-defined area or the entire drawing area.

14. T F Metafiles are used by computers to store sounds.

15. T F Draw software creates images with the use of vector graphics.

16.   T   F   Showing the changes that take place as one image is modified to become an entirely different image is called morphing.
17.   T   F   The paint roller tool in Microsoft's Paintbrush graphics application is normally used to color the background of the drawing area.
18.   T   F   Raster software uses paint graphics to create images.
19.   T   F   When the brush tool is active in Microsoft's Paintbrush graphics application, the background color is drawn at the graphics cursor position.
20.   T   F   Pie graphs and bar graphs are normally associated with presentation graphics.
21.   T   F   Most professional disciplines have found computer-based graphics to be of little value.
22.   T   F   Due to its many limitations, CD-ROM technology is not generally considered suitable for multimedia applications.
23.   T   F   A sound card is generally considered to be absolutely essential for the full enjoyment of multimedia applications.
24.   T   F   Text-to-speech software is generally classified as multimedia support software as opposed to multimedia applications software.
25.   T   F   Authoring software is a type of multimedia applications software associated with combining sound with animation.
26.   T   F   Vector graphic images are said to be bit-mapped.
27.   T   F   Animation is accomplished by the rapid repositioning of objects on the display screen.
28.   T   F   Users who purchase multimedia upgrade components separately, experience virtually no compatibility problems with the different components.
29.   T   F   Software suites provide a cost-effective way to purchase a variety of major business applications packages or capabilities.
30.   T   F   The terms animation and motion video can be used interchangeably when discussing multimedia computer applications.

Matching *Match the following terms with the appropriate definition or characteristic by placing the letter of the matching definition or characteristic in the blank.*

31.	_____ bit-mapped	(a)	Actual analog sounds that have been digitized
32.	_____ paint software	(b)	Contains a CD-ROM drive, a sound card, multimedia software, external speakers, a microphone, and several CD-ROM titles
33.	_____ pie graph		
34.	_____ draw software	(c)	Includes most of the major business applications packages or capabilities such as communications, word processing, database, spreadsheet, etc.
35.	_____ metafile		
36.	_____ vector graphics	(d)	An image projected onto the screen based on binary bits
37.	_____ multimedia upgrade kit	(e)	Lets you create multimedia applications that lets you integrate sound, motion, text, animation, and images
38.	_____ authoring software		
39.	_____ raster graphics	(f)	Contains instructions as to how to create the sound of specific instruments
40.	_____ wave files	(g)	Created with presentation graphics software using numerical data
41.	_____ software suite	(h)	Stores graphic images by using a combination of raster graphics and vector graphics
42.	_____ MIDI files	(i)	Creates an electronic canvas
		(j)	Vector graphics
		(k)	A method for maintaining a screen image as patterns of lines, points, and other shapes.
		(l)	A method for maintaining a screen image as patterns of dots.

Answers to Practice Test **1** c, **2** d, **3** b, **4** a, **5** d, **6** c, **7** b, **8** d, **9** a, **10** b, **11** c, **12** d, **13** t, **14** f, **15** t, **16** t, **17** t, **18** f, **19** f, **20** t, **21** f, **22** f, **23** t, **24** t, **25** f, **26** f, **27** t, **28** f, **29** t, **30** f, **31** d, **32** i, **33** g, **34** j, **35** h, **36** k, **37** e, **38** b, **39** l, **40** a, **41** c, **42** f.

CHAPTER CHECKUP

NAME		DATE	CHAPTER 9
COURSE	SECTION	INSTRUCTOR	

1. Name five common capabilities of graphics software and briefly discuss each. *See section 9-2 of the text.*

-

-

-

-

-

2. Depending on the software and hardware you are using, graphic images are maintained as raster graphics, vector graphics or metafiles. What are the fundamental differences between raster graphics and vector graphics and how are metafiles related to raster and vector graphics? *One deals with dots, one deals with numbers and mathematical formulas, and one deals with both. See section 9-2 of the text.*

3. Briefly describe the similarities between paint software and the traditional canvas and paints used by an artist. *See section 9-2 of the text.*

4. Briefly describe the fundamental differences between paint software and draw software. *See section 9-2 of the text.*

5. List and describe the use for five of the tools in the Paintbrush tool box. *Paintbrush is a paint software package distributed with Microsoft Windows. An image of a similar toolbox is included in the Graphical User Interface exercise for this chapter. See section 9-2 of the text.*

■

■

■

■

■

6. Discuss morphing techniques and how they are applied to computer graphics. *The term morphing is derived from the word metamorphosis and involves photographic images. See section 9-2 of the text.*

7. Discuss ways besides morphing that photo illustration software can be used to alter photographic images. *Think of all the things that can be done to alter a photograph. Don't forget about the simple things. See section 9-2 of the text.*

8. How might a marketing manager make use of the capabilities of presentation graphics? *Marketing managers are interested in sales patterns. See section 9-2 of the text.*

9. By using presentation graphics software, you can create many types of graphs and charts. List one type of graph, other than pie and bar graphs, and one type of chart. *Read about presentation graphics in section 9-3 of the text.*

■

■

10. Discuss how you can use computer graphics to enhance your resume. *See section 9-2 of the text.*

11. Describe how animation is achieved with a personal computer and monitor. *Animation relates to objects such as cartoon characters you see on TV. The same principles apply to computers as do to TV and movies. See section 9-2 of the text.*

12. Describe five hardware items you will need to take advantage of multimedia computer applications. *Multimedia involves the integration of such things as sound and motion video output into an application. See section 9-3 of the text.*

■

■

■

■

■

13. Describe the differences between multimedia support software and multimedia applications software. *This is active multimedia creation versus multimedia participation. See section 9-3 of the text.*

14. List and describe the use of five hardware or software items you would use in developing your own multimedia application. *Refer to Chapter Checkup questions five and six for this chapter to help you answer this question. See section 9-3 of the text.*

■

■

■

■

■

15. How do you think computer-based multimedia applications will impact education? *Could this be the beginning of the end to classrooms for self-motivated students?   See section 9-3 of the text.*

16. Describe the similarities and differences between images, animation, and motion video. *All may be used in a multimedia application, but each involves the use of different imaging hardware, software, and techniques.   See section 9-3 of the text.*

17. Discuss the differences between a wave file and a MIDI file. *One is digital recordings and the other is instructions.   See section 9-3 of the text.*

18. Explain how you would use a database in a multimedia application on CD-ROM. *Database applications aren't just for text and numbers anymore.   See section 9-3 of the text.*

19. List and briefly describe the various software packages that are included in a software suite with which you are familiar. (If necessary, visit a software vendor to familiarize yourself with a software suite.) *Examples of software suites to choose from are SmartSuite (Lotus), Microsoft Office Professional (see Figure 9-13) and PerfectOffice (Novell).   See section 9-4 of the text.*

20. Compose a multiple-choice, a true/false, and an essay question that you think would be appropriate for a quiz on this chapter.

M/C:
(a)
(b)
(c)
(d)
T/F:
Essay:

GRAPHICAL USER INTERFACE

Identify the items pictured below. Hint: A and B represent typefaces and fonts. Which is which? C and E represent software products. Use their names to identify which type of product: word processing, desktop publishing, or graphics.

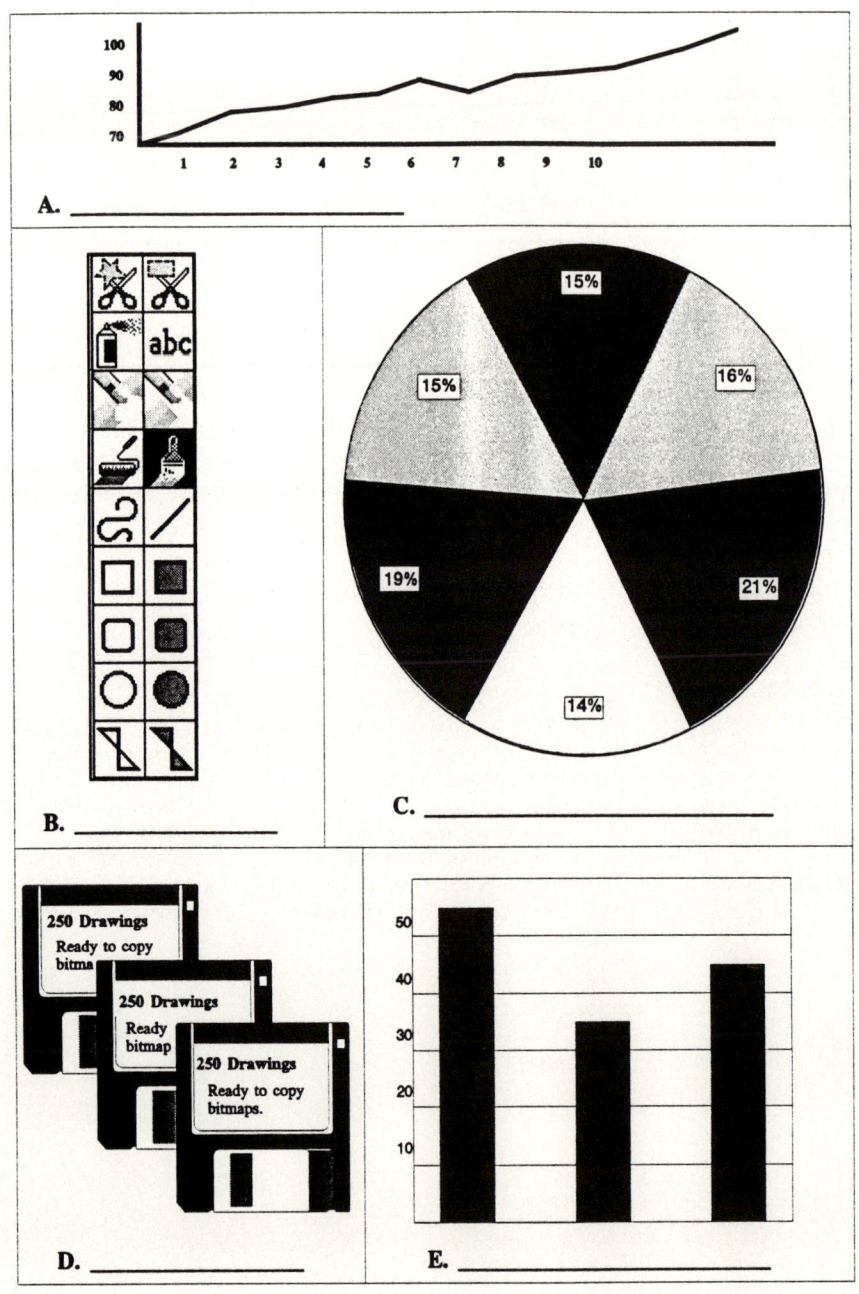

A. _____

B. _____

C. _____

D. _____

E. _____

**Chapter 10
Information Systems:
    The MIS, DSS, and EIS**

STUDENT LEARNING OBJECTIVES

- To describe how information needs vary at each level of organizational activity.
- To distinguish between programmed decisions and nonprogrammed decisions.
- To identify the elements, scope, and capabilities of an information system.
- To describe the circumstances appropriate for batch and transaction-oriented data entry.
- To define data processing system, management information system, decision support system, executive information system, expert system, and software agent.
- To identify characteristics associated with data processing systems, management information systems, decision support systems, executive information systems, expert systems, and software agents.

VOCABULARY STUDY

assistant system
batch processing
data processing (DP) system
decision support system (DSS)
exception report
executive information system
(EIS)
expert system

filtering
function-based information
system
information-based decision
integrated information system
knowledge-based system
management information system
(MIS)

nonprogrammed decision
programmed decision
software agent
source data
source document
throwaway system
transaction-oriented processing

INTERACTIVE REVIEW

Use the terms in the Vocabulary Study to fill in the following blanks. You will only use each term once. You may need to insert a plural form of a term or adjust its verb tense. Check your answers with the chapter material and the glossary in your textbook.

10-1

Today's global economy demands that managers seek strategies that can give their companies the competitive advantage. These strategies often involve computers and information technology. In this highly competitive era, the judicious use of available technology can make the difference between profitability and failure. In many cases, the return on the information technology dollar exceeds 50%.

10-2

The four primary resources of business are people, materials, money, and information. Information is still developing as a resource. It is necessary for managers to use all the resources at their disposal more effectively, meet corporate objectives, and perform the management functions of planning, organizing, leading, and controlling. The business system acts in concert with several entities, for example, employees, customers, and suppliers. Getting the right information to the right decision maker at the right time in the right form is commonly known as _ _ _ _ _ _ _ _ _ .

The four levels of information activity within a company are strategic, tactical, operational, and clerical. Most data are processed at the clerical level, and decisions made at this level are virtually all _ . Operational level tasks span one day to three months and information requirements are often operational feedback. _ _ _ _ _ _ _ _ _ _ _ _ _ _ _ _ _ _ _ , which highlight critical information, are commonly requested at this level. Tactical level information requirements are usually periodic with occasional one-time and "what if" reports. Concern is primarily with operations and budgets from year to year, and decision information is seldom conclusive. Usually, _ which are encountered at this level of management require personal judgment and intuition, and are made in conjunction with available information. Strategic level information system requirements are often one-time reports, "what if" reports, and trend analyses with decision information generally inconclusive. Unstructured problems come into play when making _ _ _ _ _ _ _ _ _ _ - _ _ _ _ _ _ _ _ _ _ _ _ _ .

10-3

An information system combines hardware, software, people, procedures, and data to provide data processing and information. An information system is capable of input, processing, storage and output. It can accept source data, an inquiry, a response to a prompt, an instruction, a message from another system, and a change. It can sort, access, record, update, summarize, select, and manipulate data. An IS can store data, text, images, and other digital information for future recall and use, and it can produce hard copy, and soft copy output and exert control over devices. A _ _ _ _ _ _ _ _ - _ _ _ _ _ _ _ _ _ _ _ _ _ _ _ _ _ _ _ is designed to support a specific application area. An _ shares a common database and provides a resource that can be shared by several application areas.

Hardware and software are said to be on-line when they can be accessed by the processor, and off-line when they cannot. _ _ _ _ _ _ _ _ _ _ are the original data entered into an IS for processing. How it is collected determines whether it has to be transcribed or can be directly entered into the system. When transcribing data from a _ _ _ _ _ _ _ _ _ _ _ _ _ _ , the terminal displays a prompt or message to the operator describing what should be entered. Both transcription and source data automation are used in _ _ _ _ _ _ _ _ _ _ _ _ _ _ and _ _ _ _ _ _ _ _ _ _ _ _ - _ _ _ _ _ _ _ _ _ _ _ _ _ _ _ _ . The major difference between the two processing methods is that in batch processing, the system is updated periodically, and in the other, the system is updated continuously.

10-4

____ _____ _____ or __ _____ deal with transaction handling and record-keeping for a particular functional area. They are characterized as being inflexible with information production primarily for operational-level activities.

10-5

A _____ _____ _____ or ___ , is an integrated structure of databases and information flow that optimizes the collection, transfer, and presentation of information throughout a multilevel organization. The organization is comprised of component groups that perform a variety of tasks to accomplish a united objective. MIS is characterized as supporting data processing, using an integrated database, supporting several functional areas, providing all management levels with timely but structured information, and improving data security. Compare this with a DP system.

10-6

_____ _____ _____ (___) assist in decision making with user-friendly hardware and software. Where the MIS is oriented toward assisting structured decision situations in limited areas, the DSS is oriented toward assisting semistructured and unstructured decision situations in any environment. In addition, the DSS is more flexible and adaptable than is the MIS, provides the decision maker with significant analytical tools, and provides portability of data and information. The DSS tool box contains a variety of hardware and software tools. The ease with which many DSS applications can be created has lead to the development of _____ _____ to support a one-time decision. Other DSS software are designed to facilitate data management. This software allows the decision maker to import data from the corporate database, and export DSS data for use by other programs. Additional DSS software tools include modeling, statistical analysis, planning, inquiry, graphics, consolidations, and application-specific DSS capabilities. The _____ _____ _____ or ___ is considered a subset of DSS and is designed to support executive level decision making.

10-7

Expert systems research and development is closely related to artificial intelligence. An _____ _____ combines preset IF-THEN rules with heuristic knowledge and factual knowledge from a domain expert to assist individuals in analysis and decision making within a narrowly defined subject area. The highest form of a sophisticated _____-____ _____ , expert systems attempt to simulate the human thought process. The less sophisticated knowledge-based systems are called _____ _____ . Assistant systems are usually implemented to reduce the possibility that the end user will make an error in judgment rather than to resolve a particular problem. The idea behind an expert system is to capture and distribute the specialized knowledge from one or more individuals in a specific, critical area of operations. Expert systems can improve the productivity and performance of decision makers, provide stability and consistency to a particular area of decision making, reduce dependencies on critical personnel, and be an excellent training tool. Expert systems are being developed for applications in a wide range of subjects, professions, and avocations.

10-8

In cyberland, _____ _____ will "live" in our computer systems and assist us with the chores of life, both at home and at work. We set the goals for our agents and the agents act to reach those goals. The agent may remain in continuous motion working toward an ongoing goal, perform an action when a specified event occurs, or perform actions needed to accomplish a one-time goal. As we evolve to an environment in which PCs are perpetually on-line, look for software agents to take on an ever increasing workload.

PRACTICE TEST

Multiple Choice *Circle the most appropriate answer.*

1. Which of these is not one of the basic elements of an information system?
   a. hardware
   b. people
   c. software
   d. DSS

2. A function-based information system
   a. is designed to support a specific application area.
   b. relies on the full integration of the database.
   c. reduces redundant data.
   d. is independent of other systems.

3. A computer system that aids the decision-making process through the use of a knowledge base is
   a. not yet available with today's technology.
   b. called an expert system.
   c. known as computer-aided manufacturing.
   d. a management information system.

4. Which of the following is the least likely information requirement at the strategic level?
   a. "what if" reports
   b. trend analyses
   c. operational feedback
   d. one-time reports

5. Which of the following is not an information system processing capability?
   a. summarizing
   b. manipulating
   c. accessing
   d. expanding

6. Which of the following is a benefit of an expert system?
   a. provides stability and consistency to decision makers
   b. decreases performance of decision makers
   c. works well as a CBT tool
   d. increases dependency on critical personnel

7. A management information system
   a. is not concerned with decision-making support.
   b. generally supports several functional areas.
   c. is primarily concerned with unstructured information.
   d. is a set of decision support tools.

8. A DP system
   a. optimizes the collection, transfer, and presentation of information throughout an organization through an integrated structure of databases and information flow.
   b. is primarily concerned with transaction handling and record-keeping, usually for a particular functional area.
   c. is an interactive information system that relies on an integrated set of user-friendly hardware and software tools to produce and present information targeted to support management in the decision-making process.
   d. is designed specifically to support decision making at the executive levels of management, primarily the tactical and strategic levels.

9. Which of the following is a group of software DSS tools?
   a. modeling, graphics, word processing
   b. data management, organizing, planning
   c. modeling, graphics, application development
   d. data management, organizing, controlling
10. Seeing that the right information reaches the right decision maker at the right time in the right form is a description of
    a. faultering.
    b. a throwaway system.
    c. an assistant system.
    d. filtering.
11. Programmed decisions are often determined by
    a. existing policies or procedures.
    b. bad decisions.
    c. computer programs.
    d. committees.
12. Computer programs which act as intermediaries, filtering the never-ending stream of information to give us only that which we need and want are referred to as
    a. software assistants.
    b. software agents.
    c. software analysts.
    d. software applicants.

True - False *Circle T for true and F for false.*

13. T F At the operational level, managers complete specific tasks as directed by tactical-level managers.
14. T F When transactions are grouped together for processing, they are said to be transaction-oriented.
15. T F DSSs are designed to support unstructured problems.
16. T F A decision support system is fundamentally the same as an uninterruptible power source.
17. T F Non-programmed decisions are also called information-based decisions.
18. T F Programmed decisions more often than not involve ill-defined problems.
19. T F DSSs are interactive.
20. T F Generally, throwaway systems are used and reused many times over several years before being discarded.
21. T F Data processing capabilities are provided by an information system.
22. T F MIS is a commonly used acronym for "management information security".
23. T F Expert systems can be employed to provide better service and increase productivity.
24. T F An expert system would not be considered a knowledge-based system.
25. T F Exception reports highlight critical information and are often requested by tactical and strategic level managers.
26. T F An MIS is designed and created to support a specific application or set of applications.
27. T F DSS applications are often developed to help with a particular decision or set of decisions and are then discarded.
28. T F A software agent performs actions needed to accomplish a one-time goal.
29. T F In the short period of their existence, expert systems have operated unimpressively and they have failed to improve.
30. T F Assistant systems are the most advanced form of expert system.

Matching *Match the following terms with the appropriate definition or characteristic by placing the letter of the matching definition or characteristic in the blank.*

31.	_____nonprogrammed decision	(a)	At this level, managers are concerned with operations and budgets from year to year
32.	_____DP system	(b)	A less sophisticated knowledge-based system that helps users make straight-forward decisions
33.	_____source document		
34.	_____ domain expert	(c)	Decision maker has no judgmental flexibility in making the decision
35.	_____ executive support system	(d)	Reports that highlight critical information
		(e)	Information-based decisions
36.	_____ programmed decision	(f)	The foundation of an operational expert system
37.	_____tactical level of activity	(g)	At this level, people are concerned primarily with transaction handling
38.	_____ exception report	(h)	Systems that share a common database
39.	_____ integrated information system	(i)	Designed to support decision making at the tactical and strategic levels of management
40.	_____ clerical level of activity	(j)	A form containing data for computer entry
41.	_____ assistant system	(k)	Provides the factual knowledge and the heuristic rules for input to a knowledge base.
42.	_____ knowledge base	(l)	Cannot accommodate data processing or information needs not already built into the system

Answers to Practice Test **1** d, **2** a, **3** b, **4** c, **5** d, **6** a, **7** b, **8** c, **9** d, **10** a, **11** b, **12** b, **13** t, **14** f, **15** t, **16** f, **17** t, **18** f, **19** t, **20** f, **21** t, **22** f, **23** t, **24** f, **25** t, **26** f, **27** t, **28** t, **29** f, **30** f, **31** e, **32** l, **33** j, **34** k, **35** i, **36** c, **37** a, **38** d, **39** h, **40** g, **41** b, **42** f.

CHAPTER CHECKUP

NAME		DATE	CHAPTER 10
COURSE	SECTION	INSTRUCTOR	

1. Discuss the relationship, if any, between information systems and a company's competitive advantage in the marketplace? *See section 10-1 of the text.*

2. Why do well-designed information systems filter information? Give an example to illustrate your answer. *Making sense of information is as important as the information itself. See section 10-2 of the text.*

3. Associate the following items or characteristics with the appropriate level of organizational activity (Clerical, Operational, Tactical, and Strategic). *See section 10-3 of the text.*

(a) on-line order entry

(b) repetitive tasks

(c) what if reports

(d) biweekly individual sales report

(e) processing product orders

(f) projected production for the coming year

(g) long-term sales trend graphs.

4. Examine Figure 10-2 in the text and describe how the sales trend for Alphas differs from the sales trend for Deltas. *See section 10-2 of the text.*

5. Give a real-world example of a programmed decision. *For example, the awarding of letter grades to students can be programmed based on preset overall percentage criteria. See section 10-2 of the text.*

6. What five elements are combined to make an information system? *Don't confuse with capabilities. One of them is hardware. See section 10-3 of the text.*

■

■

■

■

■

7. How is a function-based information system different from an integrated information system? *See section 10-3 of the text.*

8. List two examples of data and two examples of hardware that are off-line. *See section 10-3 of the text.*

Data:
■

■

Hardware:
■

■

9. List two examples of data and two examples of hardware that are on-line. *See section 10-3 of the text.*

Data:
■

■

Hardware:
■

■

10. List two advantages that transaction-oriented processing has over batch processing. *See section 10-3 of the text.*

■

■

11. Give a general description of a source document you have completed during the past year. Be sure you include all the various types of information on this source document. *For example: survey questionnaires or health forms. See section 10-3 of the text.*

12. Name three desirable characteristics of an MIS. *There are five listed in the text. See section 10-5 of the text.*

■

■

■

13. Name two ways in which a DSS is different from an MIS. *DSS stands for Decision Support System and MIS for Management Information System. Remember structured verses unstructured decisions. See section 10-6 of the text.*

■

■

14. What, if any, is the difference between an executive information system and a decision support system? *See section 10-6 of the text.*

15. How is the DSS tool box helpful to managers? Name two software DSS tools. *See section 10-6 of the text.*

■

■

16. What is the primary drawback of a basic data processing system? *See section 10-4 of the text.*

17. Name and describe two characteristics of an environment that make it conducive for an expert system. *See section 10-7 of the text.*

■

■

18. Briefly discuss the basic differences between an assistant system and an expert system. *See section 10-7 of the text.*

19. List and briefly describe three ways a software agent reacts to meet the demands of a specified goal and discuss a real life example of each. *A software agent has the authority to act on our behalf, just as a human agent. We set goals for our agents and the agents act to reach those goals. How can you make use of a personal assistant in your daily routine? See section 10-8 of the text.*

■

■

■

20.   Compose a multiple-choice, a true/false, and an essay question that you think would be appropriate for a quiz on this chapter.

M/C:

(a)

(b)

(c)

(d)

T/F:

Essay:

GRAPHICAL USER INTERFACE

Associate each of the following DSS capabilities with one or more DSS software tools illustrated in the DSS toolbox below.

_____	Drill down
_____	What if
_____	Pie graph
_____	Collection of like data
_____	Exporting DSS data
_____	Used when several outcomes are anticipated
_____	Goal seeking
_____	Quality control system
_____	Permits queries to database
_____	Import from mainframe-based DBMS
_____	Throwaway system
_____	Regression analysis

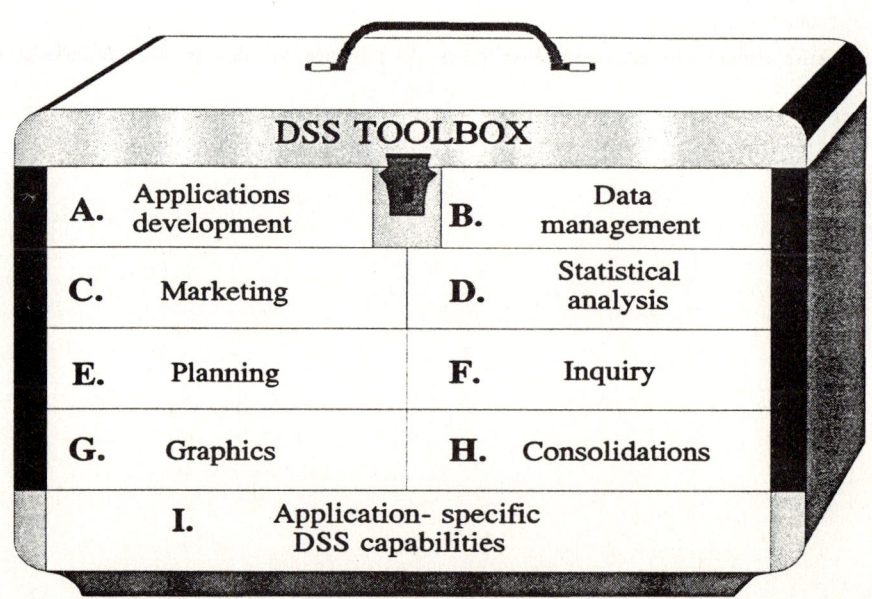

DSS TOOLBOX

A. Applications development

B. Data management

C. Marketing

D. Statistical analysis

E. Planning

F. Inquiry

G. Graphics

H. Consolidations

I. Application- specific DSS capabilities

**Chapter 11
Computers in Society**

STUDENT LEARNING OBJECTIVES

- To become aware of the relationship between career mobility and computer knowledge.
- To identify ergonomic and environmental considerations in the design of the knowledge worker's work place.
- To identify points of security vulnerability for a computer center, an information system, and a PC.
- To explore ethical questions concerning the use of information technology.

VOCABULARY STUDY

acomputer matching
computer monitoring
cryptography
encryption/decryption
ergonomics

fault-tolerant
footprint
logical security
physical security
pilferage

software piracy
uninterruptible power source (UPS)

INTERACTIVE REVIEW

Use the terms in the Vocabulary Study to fill in the following blanks. You will only use each term once. You may need to insert a plural form of a term or adjust its verb tense. Check your answers with the chapter material and the glossary in your textbook.

11-1

The virtual frontier may be the last great frontier. Much of what lies beyond the virtual horizon is uncharted and potentially dangerous territory. The virtual frontier encompasses the electronic highways that comprise the Internet, thousands of BBSs, scores of information services, and thousands of private networks. The information superhighway metaphor is frequently used as a collective reference to the electronic links that have wired our world. Electronic outlaws may have their way in the virtual frontier until cybercops armed with strict cyberlaws drive them out. The important thing to remember is that the information superhighway is truly a frontier that may not be tamed in the foreseeable future.

11-2

Jobs for computer specialists are increasing every year. The computer systems analyst job has been called the best job in America, followed by physician, physical therapist, electrical engineer, and civil engineer. Every facet of automation is moving ever closer to those who use it. Computer competency is already a prerequisite employment in many professions. Eventually, virtually every job will require some degree of computer competency.

11-3

_ _ _ _ _ _ _ _ _ _ is the study of the relationships between people and the machines. Its goal for knowledge workers is to design a workplace that is safe, comfortable, effective, and efficient. The safety aspect of ergonomics involves addressing both sudden accidental injuries and cumulative injuries that manifest themselves over long periods of time. The problems associated with VODS are not exclusive to the syndrome, but they are still real and require the attention of managers just the same. As the number of repetitive-stress injuries (RSIs) increased for knowledge workers, workstation ergonomics became an increasingly important issue for corporate productivity. A poorly designed workplace for the knowledge worker has the potential to cause CTD which can be permanently debilitating for the employee and expensive for the employer. The key to designing a proper work place for the knowledge worker is flexibility. Both ANSI and OSHA are involved in research, design, and regulation of the knowledge workers workplace to reduce and avoid injury.

The subject of green computing encompasses a wide area of subjects. The EPAs Energy Star guidelines set forth several energy saving standards for computers and peripherals. Other recommendations by green computing proponents include printing only what needs to be printed; buying equipment from vendors who are manufacturing environmentally safe products; purchasing recycled paper; recycling paper and printer toner cartridges (which would probably end up in landfills); buying reconditioned components rather than new ones; recycling old PCs and printers; shopping electronically to save gas; and telecommuting once or twice a week.

11-4

The computer revolution has generated intense controversy in the area of what is and is not ethical with regard to activities involving information technology. A code of ethics similar to the one in the text provides a good base regarding the ethical conduct of computer professionals. Vast amounts of personal data on identifiable individuals are contained in numerous private and government databases around the country. The safeguarding of that information is a serious problem for computer professionals. Often, what is one person's legitimate use of this data is another person's invasion of privacy. A good example of this is comparing two or more databases to find individuals which are common to each. This procedure is called _ _ _ _ _ _ _ _ _ _ _ _ . A medical researcher may use this procedure to save lives while a con artist may use the same procedure on the same databases as the researcher to identify potential victims. Another controversial activity in the workplace is the use of computers to continuously gather and assimilate data on job activities to measure worker performance. This activity is called _ _ _ _ _ _ _ _ _ _ _ _ .

In addition to defining the proper use verses the misuse of personal information, computer crime is on the rise. Legislation, the criminal justice system, and industry are not yet adequately prepared to cope with it. Computer fraud involves premeditated or conscious effort to defraud a computer-based system. Negligence and incompetence can cause someone outside the organization to be unnecessarily inconvenienced, and it is usually a result of poor input/output control. Hackers have tapped into everything from local credit agencies to top-secret defense systems. The evidence of unlawful entry is called a _ _ _ _ _ _ _ _ _ . Hackers also maliciously infect computer systems with viruses. Crime on the Internet is an ever increasing problem. The Internet's cybercops, the Computer Emergency Response Team at Carnegie Mellon University, often work around the clock to thwart electronic vandalism and crime on the Internet. The unauthorized copying and use of proprietary software is called _ _ _ _ _ _ _ _ _ _ _ _ _ _ . A specific form of this where a company purchases a software product without a site-usage license agreement, then copies and distributes it throughout the company is called _ _ _ _ _ _ _ _ _ . Some employers are taking the position that theft is theft. If an employee will place their employer at risk of legal action by stealing software, then what else is this employee willing to do?

11-5

Hardware, software, files/databases, data communications, and personnel and points where a company's computer center is vulnerable to damage from unscrupulous or incompetent individuals, and from natural disaster. A network that is said to be _ _ _ _ _ - _ _ _ _ _ _ _ _ _ has duplicates of vital components on-line at all times. The degree to which a network is made fault-tolerant depends on the emphasis the organization places on its system. The effects of dirty power and power failures on computer hardware can be minimized by the use of an _ (UPS). Safeguards should also be in place to protect against unlawful modification of software and viruses. Backups of files and databases should be kept in separate locations and protected from tampering and disasters. Data that are communicated from one location to another can be protected with _ _ _ _ _ _ _ _ _ _ _ _ _ . A key is used in conjunction with _ _ _ _ _ _ _ _ _ _ _ _ _ / _ _ _ _ _ _ _ _ _ hardware to scramble and unscramble messages. Both sender and receiver must have the key, which is actually an algorithm that rearranges the bit structure of the message. Perhaps the biggest threat to the security of a company's computer system and the data which it contains is the dishonesty and/or incompetence of its own employees.

Information system security measures fall into one of two classifications. Protective measures for hardware, facilities, magnetic disks, and other items that could illegally be accessed, stolen, or destroyed are classified as _ _ _ _ _ _ _ _ _ _ _ _ _ _ _ . Passwords and user IDs are a part of the _ _ _ _ _ _ _ _ _ _ _ _ _ that can be built into software. Security frequently is the responsibility of the individual users who may or may not have security training. The most frequently used physical PC security tools include the lock and key and the badge reader. Multimedia systems equipped with the proper software can use voice prints to add an extra layer of security. Some people place a special filter over the screen that permits only straight-on viewing. Passwords and user IDs remain the foundation of logical PC security. The user ID is your electronic identifier and may be known by your friends and colleagues. The password, however, is yours alone to protect and use.

11-6

The dynamics of a rapidly advancing computer technology demand constant updating of skills and expertise. The total amount of computing capacity in the world is doubling every two years. The level at which you participate in the computer revolution and the impact it has on society is up to you. Your future is in your hands, and the quality of that future will be substantially affected by computers.

PRACTICE TEST

Multiple Choice *Circle the letter of the most appropriate answer.*

1. Headaches, depression, anxiety, nausea, fatigue, and irritability associated with extended use of a terminal or PC are collectively referred to as
    a. VODS.
    b. ISDN.
    c. CTD.
    d. VDTS.

2. When a company purchases or leases a software package, they usually receive
    a. one free year of technical support.
    b. computer hardware.
    c. a license agreement.
    d. special chips to help them use the software.

3. Job performance of employees is sometimes analyzed by employers using
    a. computer switching.
    b. computer matching.
    c. computer catching.
    d. computer monitoring.

4. Searching separate databases to identify individuals common to both is called
    a. computer monitoring.
    b. computer melding.
    c. computer matching.
    d. computer masking.

5. Computer crimes are
    a. almost always detected.
    b. often not reported.
    c. very rare and easily detected.
    d. impossible to commit.

6. The unlawful duplication of proprietary software is called
    a. software porting.
    b. software virus.
    c. software monitoring.
    d. software piracy.

7. An organization at Carnegie Mellon University that works to thwart electronic vandalism and crime on the Internet is referred to as
    a. CERT.
    b. CRET.
    c. CTRT.
    d. CTRE.

8. Companies address the threat of unauthorized access to data communications with
    a. cryptography techniques.
    b. cartography techniques.
    c. calligraphy techniques.
    d. geography techniques.

9. Protection of hardware, facilities, magnetic disks, and other items that could be illegally accessed, stolen, or destroyed is called
    a. logical security.
    b. locality security.
    c. cryptological security.
    d. physical security.

10. A network designed to permit continuous operation, even if important components of the network fail is said to be
    a. fault-intolerant.
    b. failure-tolerant.
    c. failure intolerant.
    d. fault-tolerant.
11. Procedures that make it difficult to modify a program for purposes of personal gain are commonly called
    a. change-control procedures.
    b. operational-control procedures.
    c. design-control procedures.
    d. implementation-control procedures.
12. The biggest threat to a company's information system is
    a. infection from a computer virus.
    b. the dishonesty and/or negligence of its own employees.
    c. damage to hardware components from dirty power.
    d. overzealous hackers tapping into sensitive communications and computer systems.

True - False *Circle T next to each true statement and F next to each false statement.*

13. T F Ergonomics is the study of people and their machines.
14. T F Having several generations of backup to all files is sufficient insurance against loss of files and databases.
15. T F A poorly designed work place has the potential to cause cumulative trauma disorder.
16. T F Evidence of an unlawful entry into a computer system is called encryption.
17. T F To comply with Energy Star requirements, monitors and processors in standby mode can consume no more than 30 watts of power.
18. T F The two main causes of illegal information processing are fraud and POS terminals.
19. T F The area of computer law is growing within the legal community.
20. T F The federal government vigorously enforces strict laws enacted to regulate the sale or distribution of personal information contained in computer databases.
21. T F Negligence is defined as activities that involve a premeditated or conscious effort to defraud a computer-based system.
22. T F Software pilferage refers to the use of commercial software packages without purchasing an adequate number of site-usage license agreements.
23. T F In computer monitoring, computers continuously gather and assimilate data on consumer spending to track the activities of individuals as they occur.
24. T F Computer matching may be used as an effective law enforcement tool.
25. T F Electronic evidence of illegal or unauthorized computer activity is commonly referred to as cybertracks.
26. T F The largest threat of computer fraud to an organization is from its own employees.
27. T F Clean power for a computer is provided by what is commonly called an unincorrigible power supply.
28. T F Encryption/decryption hardware is a security measure for data communications.
29. T F It is estimated that a large bank could survive for approximately one week in the event it were to loose the use of its computer system.
30. T F Computer monitoring includes screening E-mail between employees.

Matching

Match the following terms with the appropriate definition or characteristic by placing the letter of the matching definition or characteristic in the blank.

31. ____ physical security		(a)	The evidence of unlawful entry into a computer system.
32. ____Energy Star		(b)	Repetitive stress injuries
		(c)	Cumulative trauma disorder
33. ____logical security		(d)	A program that infects other programs
34. ____ computer monitoring		(e)	The study of the relationship between people and machines.
35. ____ site license agreement		(f)	Headaches, depression, and nausea, associated with extended use of a terminal or PC
36. ____ footprint		(g)	Security measures built into software to protect against unauthorized use
37. ____cryptography		(h)	Scrambled data communications transmissions for security purposes
38. ____ergonomics		(i)	Security measures implemented to protect hardware from damage.
39. ____ impairment of motor skills		(j)	Computers continuously gather and assimilate data on job activities to measure worker performance
40. ____ RSI		(k)	The permission to use proprietary software on several computer systems
41. ____VODS		(l)	The Environmental Protection Agency
42. ____ virus			

Answers to Practice Test **1** a, **2** c, **3** d, **4** c, **5** b, **6** d, **7** a, **8** a, **9** d, **10** d, **11** a, **12** b, **13** t, **14** f, **15** t, **16** f, **17** t, **18** f, **19** t, **20** f, **21** f, **22** t, **23** f, **24** t, **25** f, **26** t, **27** f, **28** t, **29** f, **30** t, **31** i, **32** l, **33** g, **34** j, **35** k, **36** a, **37** h, **38** e, **39** c, **40** b, **41** f, **42** d.

CHAPTER CHECKUP

NAME		DATE	CHAPTER 11
COURSE	SECTION	INSTRUCTOR	

1. Discuss two health concerns surrounding the work place of the knowledge worker. *What is CTD? See section 11-3 of the text.*

-

-

2. What is Energy Star and how does it apply to information systems and society. Be specific. *Energy Star is a set of regulations and guidelines developed by the Envionmental Protection Agency that apply to computers and their peripherals. See section 11-3 of the text.*

3. Which points covered in the suggested code of ethics for computer professionals would not be applicable to other professionals? *Read through them in section 11-4 of the text and apply them to your chosen career.*

4. Should computer personnel (programmers, analysts, etc.) be held legally liable for problems with systems they develop? Why or why not? *What about CPAs and licensed professional engineers. See section 11-4 of the text.*

5. How can computer monitoring be used with telephone operators? *See section 11-4 of the text.*

6. Describe what type of personal information might be gathered about you when making a telephone call from your home. *Start with location and time of day. See section 11-4 of the text.*

7. What is the difference between the terms negligence and fraud? Give an example of each not mentioned in the text. *Review examples Review examples in section 11-4 of the text.*

8. Describe how computer matching might be used to identify tax cheaters. *Credit card purchases can be used in this type of computer activity. See section 11-4 of the text.*

9. How could computer matching be used other than in a situation of wrong doing? *A company's marketing department might find this helpful. See section 11-4 of the text.*

10. What penalties would you recommend for those who intentionally infect a computer system with a computer virus? Would you impose penalties for those who unintentionally infect a computer system with a computer virus? If so, under what circumstances? *Some malicious crackers leave much more than a footprint they infect the computer system with a computer virus. Viruses, which infect programs and databases, can be found at all levels of computing. Viruses are written by outlaw hackers and programmers to cause harm to the computer systems of unsuspecting victims. See section 11-4 of the text.*

11. What recommendations would you make for reducing criminal activity on the Internet? *The Internet's cybercops on the Computer Emergency Response Team at Carnegie Mellon University often work around the clock to thwart electronic vandalism and crime on the Internet. CERT concentrates its efforts on battling major threats to the global Internet. See section 11-4 of the text.*

12. Explain how you would feel about a manager who states bluntly that software piracy is a crime and offenders will be dismissed. *Vendors of software for personal computers estimate that for every software product sold, two more are illegally copied. Worldwide, the software industry loses an estimated 7 to 10 billion dollars a year to software piracy. See section 11-4 of the text.*

13. List the five general areas of vulnerability for a company's computer center mentioned in the text. *See section 11-5 of the text.*

■

■

■

■

■

14. Contrast the terms physical security and logical security. *See section 11-5 of the text.*

15. Describe the scope of the computer center security systems in use at your school or place of work. *Contact the Computing Services department for your school or employer. See section 11-5 of the text.*

16. Name two sources for computer viruses? *Anytime you introduce data to your computer from an outside source in an electronic format, you run the risk of encountering a virus. See section 11-5 of the text.*

■

■

17. What can you do to combat computer viruses? *Bodily harm to someone you may know who is responsible for a virus is not socially acceptable, no matter how you may feel. It's easier and a lot less of a personal hassle to use a vaccine. See section 11-5 of the text.*

18. Describe how encryption/decription technology can be used to protect data communications. *Some companies use cryptography to scramble messages sent over data communications channels. See section 11-5 of the text.*

19. Discuss reasons why you think the employees of a company would be considered as the biggest threat to the company's information system. *See section 11-5 of the text.*

20. Compose a multiple-choice, a true/false, and an essay question that you think would be appropriate for a quiz on this chapter.

M/C:
(a)
(b)
(c)
(d)
T/F:
Essay:

GRAPHICAL USER INTERFACE

Describe all of the aspects of data communications security that you see represented here.

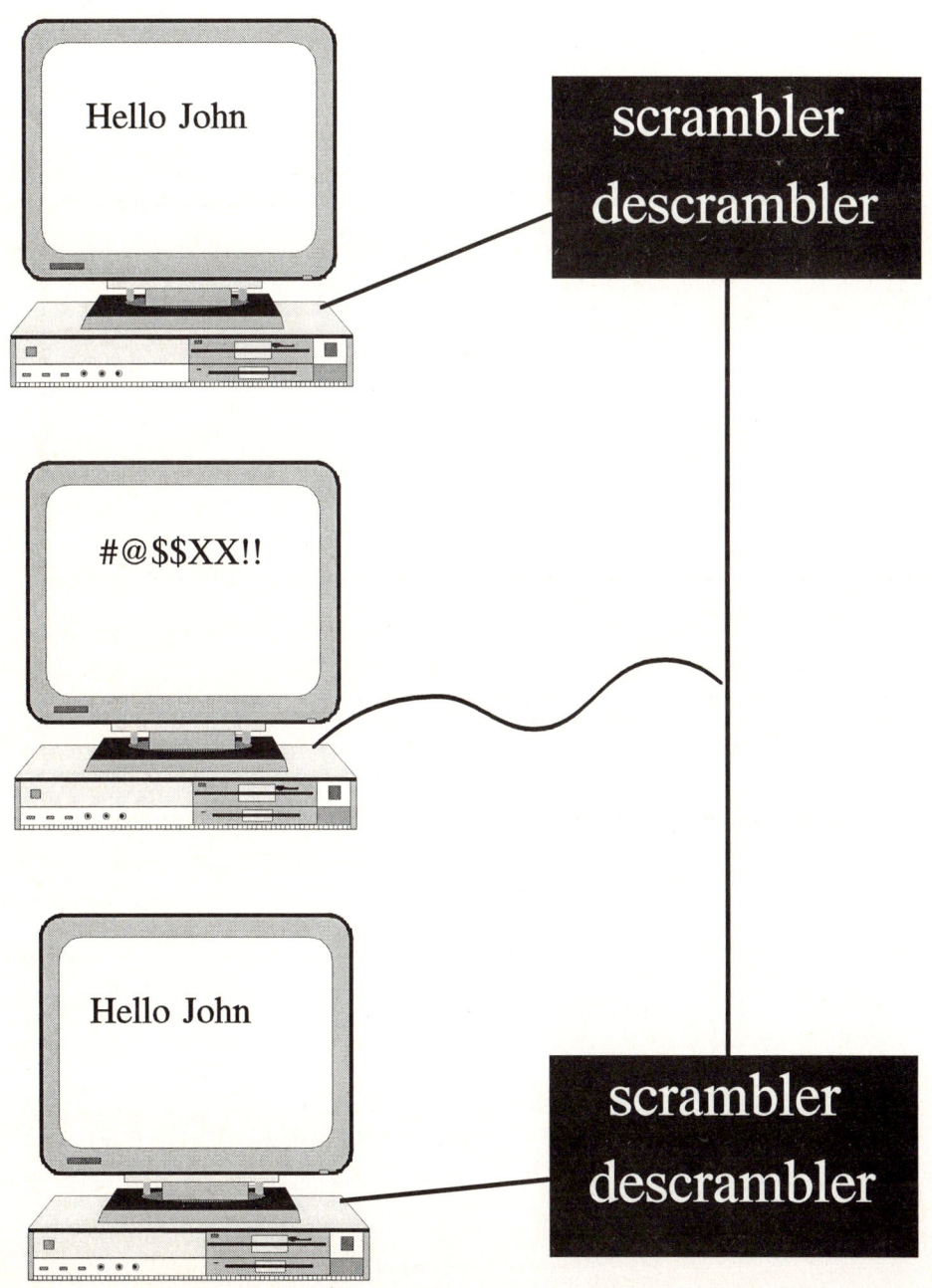